AUTUMN GOLD

Enjoying Old Age

Clifford Pond

Grace Publications Trust

GRACE PUBLICATIONS TRUST
175 Tower Bridge Road
London SE1 2AH
England

Joint Managing Editors:
J.P. Arthur MA
D.P. Kingdon MA, BD

First printed 2001

Distributed by
EVANGELICAL PRESS
Faverdale North Industrial Estate
Darlington
DL3 OPH
England

British Library Cataloguing in Publication Data available

ISBN 0 946462-60-7

Printed and bound in Great Britain by:
Creative Print & Design Wales, Ebbw Vale

AUTUMN GOLD

Enjoying Old Age

DEDICATION

To Georgie with my love

ACKNOWLEDGEMENTS

I am very grateful to the many people who have helped me to write this book, especially to those senior citizens who have more experience of the subject than I have known as yet, and to staff and residents of Pilgrim Homes.

CONTENTS

FOREWORD

My work at Pilgrim Homes, a charity that cares for elderly Christians, has made me realise that there is a great need for a book that provides biblical and practical counsel for the elderly. When a resident comes into one of our homes and a pastor writes a helpful and encouraging letter, we are so pleased. I have often wished that their pastoral advice could be put into book form so that it can be shared with other elderly Christians. In *Autumn Gold* Clifford Pond has done just that.

I have greatly enjoyed reading this book. I am quite certain that Christians, both old and young, will greatly benefit from doing so as well. Practical issues that elderly Christians have to face, such as keeping fit, are helpfully and sensitively dealt with, and in a way that will also guide family and friends in how to relate to senior citizens. The Scriptures are applied in a relevant and encouraging way, demonstrating how it is possible — and important — to *enjoy* God in old age.

Clifford Pond's style is easy to read and he has certainly blazed a trail in an area that needs attention. He has set a standard against which all other books of this nature will be compared. More importantly, he has provided elderly Christians with an invaluable resource to which they can refer again and again for advice and comfort. I wish *Autumn Gold* every success.

Peter Tervet, Chief Executive, Pilgrim Homes

INTRODUCTION

'What', I hear you say, 'does a youngster like you know about old age? You are only 75!

Well, I admit, if you are 85 you have a lot to teach me, but consider this. If I were any younger I would have little or nothing to say, but if I get much older I'll not be able to write a book. So you see, now seems to be the right time.

Then I have additional qualifications. Despite appearances, I could show you the tell tale signs of age. I can be seen regularly leaving the local chemists with my repeat prescription for treating blood pressure and glaucoma. If I neglect my exercises, a disc soon slips and I quickly join the clan of stiff-necked people. Furthermore, an increasing number of names of people and places dodge in and stay out of my memory (never notably efficient) and time doesn't just fly, it just seems to glide past unnoticed! You recognise the symptoms don't you? Oh! I have just remembered. I am a great grandfather now! Lastly, I meet the first of Frank Muir's and Denis Norden's three qualifications for old age status — you do not kneel down unless you have first spotted something you can grab to pull yourself up again! [1]

Why a book about old age? One reason is that as I was considering whether my writing days were over, I began to feel that this is what the Lord wanted me to do. The words of Psalm 92, verses 12-14, just wouldn't go away.

> 'The righteous will flourish like a palm tree, they will grow like a cedar of Lebanon; planted in the house of the LORD, they will flourish in the courts of our God. They will still bear fruit in old age, they will stay fresh and green ... '

Then, enquiry showed that apart from one booklet by David Gay, and one other book on the stocks by Roger Hitchings, there is little or nothing available in the book shops on this subject. This is strange, when you remember that the number of older people in society is growing rapidly year by year. A CARE action file says, 'More and more people in Britain are surviving to old age. The chances of someone living beyond age 75 are better now than they have ever been. Increased longevity is one of the greatest achievements of the 20th century ... ' In 1968, there were 340 people over 100 years old in the world; in 1988 this number had risen to 34,000. In 1999 16% of British households consisted of pensioners living alone. Surely Christians have something important to say in this situation! Certainly the Bible is by no means silent about the blessings and challenges of old age. Our forefathers talked a lot about ageing and dying but were quiet about sex. Nowadays there is an obsession with sex but ageing and dying are forbidden subjects except for comedians or as social or economic problems.

I am very much aware of the wide range of ages and conditions covered by expressions like 'advancing years' or 'those who are ageing'. The retired population can range from fit people who retire at 55 to those who are clinging on to life at 80+ or 90+. So in this book there will be chapters that do not apply to you; in that case why not pray for those you know to whom they do relate. I hope all my readers will find themselves somewhere in the book, and that what is said will be helpful. All kinds of things have been written by psychologists and sociologists about old age, and there are magazines like 'Saga' that specifically address the needs that arise. Helpful literature is also available from Age Concern and Help the Aged. Much of this is interesting and helpful in the areas of physical, material and financial needs, but a Christian approach has a spiritual dimension that gives light and colour to everything else.

As I thought about this distinctively Christian approach based on the Bible, I realised that, in the process, I was helping myself. I was being reminded of things I myself am in danger of forgetting and I was being corrected where already I am failing. I hope this book will do you as much good as it is doing me!

Most of what has been written elsewhere has been addressed to society at large, or churches, stressing their responsibilities to other people. This is necessary and valuable, but my purpose here is to speak to older people themselves. There is so much we can do to help ourselves in order to be a blessing in the world and not a burden.

There is no doubt that if we honour the Lord as our years advance, we are making a significant contribution to the total evangelistic thrust of the churches. No-one makes a greater impact on others than a Christian who, as we say, grows old graciously.

I have two pictures in mind; both are of sunsets. The one is obviously beautiful with its blazing colours filling the western sky. As the sun sets on our short lives, we surely want the beauty of Jesus to be reflected through us to the end.

The other picture is of a stormy, glowering sky, frowning with dark colours and full of threatening and foreboding. An artist sees beauty here too, where others turn away their faces and pull down the shutters. Without faith we see little or no good in an ageing life, heavy with burdens and wrestling with sickness and pain. Yet like the artist, the eye of faith can see a beauty here also where child-like trust and hopeful joy refuse to be crushed. The message is for all in every or any situation, glad or sad. Christ is the answer to every need — right to the very end of life.

---

[1] 'A Kentish Lad' by Frank Muir, page 397.

BEATITUDES FOR THE AGED

Blessed are they who understand
My faltering step and palsied hand.
Blessed are they who know my ears today
Must strain to catch the things they say.
Blessed are they who seem to know
My eyes are dim and wits are slow.
Blessed are they who look away
When coffee was spilt on the table today.
Blessed are they with a cheery smile,
Who stop to chat for a little while.
Blessed are they who never say,
'You've told that story twice today'.
Blessed are they who know the way
To bring back memories of yesterday.
Blessed are they who make it known
I'm loved, respected, and not alone.
Blessed are they who ease the days
On my journey home in loving ways.

(Taken from *Whittlesey Baptist Church 'News'*, Harvest Edition, 1999).

CHAPTER ONE

No Shame!

Some years ago (I'm reminiscing — I'm ageing!), I had to leave home early on Sunday mornings to conduct services in different parts of the country. Soon after leaving town there would be the quiet country lanes, and then every so often I would meet the 'joggers'. Some were young and strong with a spring in their firm strides. Others were bent low, breathing heavily, with knobbly knees and laboured tread. I wondered if they had suddenly realised that they were getting old and were looking for the shortest route into eternity!

Why did they do it? Perhaps someone had convinced them that jogging would save them from heart disease, and they had a genuine wish to remain well as long as possible. Whatever the reason, there is no doubt that somewhere in their thoughts was a horror of growing old and a desire to stave it off as long as possible.

Perhaps you say, 'those people may be misguided, but there is something natural and reasonable in what they are trying to do'. I agree that it is quite right for us to keep as well as we can for our own sake as well as for the sake of those who have to care for us if we become ill, but it is another thing to act as though there was some kind of shame in getting old. We surely must avoid the cynicism that says, 'An aged man is but a paltry thing, a tattered coat upon a stick ... ' (W.B. Yeats).

We should not try to deceive ourselves and others that we are not as old as we really are. Why do some people resent any reference to their age? Why do older men try to convince themselves that they are still young by wearing young men's fashions and sporting trendy hairstyles? Why do some women in their sixties still think that they can turn the heads of young men?

Why do others rush to the chemist for hair dye, not to speak of acquiring a wig as soon as a few flecks of grey begin to appear? They do not want to face the obvious fact that age is beginning to take its toll.

A true Christian attitude to age advance is not so much 'ah well, I suppose there is nothing I can do about it, so I must make the best of it', as 'this is God's will for me, so he has a good purpose which will be for his glory. There may be much in the future I will not enjoy, but I will accept it and submit to it for his sake'.

That may seem to you to be difficult to say with sincerity. If so, reflect on this. As we read the stories of how people died as martyrs, we are astonished that many of them had the grace and strength to embrace the stake at which they were burned as a kind of privilege to suffer for the Lord's sake. You and I may suffer a great deal, but we can say to ourselves 'if that is how those people welcomed their sufferings that were so much greater than mine, then I am willing to accept what God has for me in the days ahead and use it for his praise'.

Another evidence of unwillingness to come to terms with ageing is the fact that we rarely discuss it in advance. I asked a number of elderly people if they had discussed the approach of old age, and most of them had not done so with the exception of a retired missionary who had often discussed it with his wife but with no-one else. It seems that most of us approach advancing years as though they should not happen.

The Old Testament story of Barzillai is very revealing. While King David was in exile, this man, who was rich, helped to provide what David needed. When the king was able to return to Jerusalem, he wanted to honour Barzillai and give him a share in his restoration, but by now Barzillai was an old man and he declined the honour protesting that he did not want to be a burden on the king and his household. He argued 'how many more years shall I live ... I am now eighty years old ... Why should your servant be an added burden to my lord the king?' (2 Samuel 19:31-37). What a self-effacing man and how well he had come to terms with his old age! There was no attitude of rebellion or bitterness, but a realistic acceptance of his situation. The priority was that the king's interests were most important and should not be hindered in any way. Our attitude must be the same as that of John the Baptist, who said of Jesus, 'He must become greater;I must become less' (John 3:30).

A hundred years ago in the *Quarterly Record* of the Pilgrim Homes, a contributor commented 'many people have a silly dread of growing old, and look upon grey hairs as a standing libel. But its Indian Summer often brings a full granary and a golden leaf ... The aged believer seems to see deeper into God's word and further into God's heaven'.

My sister, a little older than I, was in a shop recently when she saw herself in a mirror. She did not like what she saw and immediately dragged herself to Boots' to buy some ointments with a view to bringing about some improvements. What's wrong with that? Nothing! She's my sister, isn't she? It all depends on an attitude of mind. It is not only permissible, it is positively God glorifying to do the best we can 'with the material at our disposal'. But, as Christians, we should not resent what is happening to us, much less should we fight against it or even worse, complain to God about it.

Life has many curiosities and one of them is that when we are young, we try to make out that we are older than we are, and when we are ageing, we pretend that we're younger. We need to tell ourselves that just as we could not advance the clock in earlier days, so we cannot stop it now or turn it back. Jesus himself said 'Who of you by worrying can add a single hour to his life?' (Matthew 6:27), and we can properly add 'or subtract a single hour either'.The reality is more like travelling on a train and watching the evenly spaced telegraph poles go by. At first they will not go fast enough, but as the journey proceeds the poles flash past at an ever increasing rate

So let us approach advancing years as we would any other fresh challenge in life, with its opportunity to prove God's goodness and grace in the new experiences that age brings with it.

CHAPTER TWO

Always rejoice!

'Rejoice ... I will say it again; rejoice!' Who said that? Where was he? What was his situation? You might think that he was someone in the prime of life, living in reasonable comfort and with few, if any, worries. But no, these words were written by a man who was getting on in years, languishing in a Roman prison — the apostle Paul. The secret is in the words that I have omitted — 'in the Lord'. (Philippians 4:4). In other words, no matter what our circumstances may be, the Lord is always with us, assuring us of his fatherly care and sweetening every new experience.

One day not long ago, I overheard a conversation between two gentlemen, each of them bending under the weight of eighty years and more. They were discussing the words of Psalm 90:10:

> 'The length of our days is seventy years — or eighty if we have the strength, yet their span is but trouble and sorrow, for they quickly pass and we fly away.'

They agreed that each of them had known plenty about the trouble and sorrow and yet they were agreeing that these were overwhelmed by the joy they had in the Lord. Their faces showed how glad they were to be able to share this experience with each other.

The same Psalm has some rather solemn things to say about the passing years.

> 'We are consumed by your anger and terrified by your indignation. You have set our iniquities before you, our secret sins in the light of your presence. All our days pass away under your wrath; we finish our years with a moan' (Verses 7-9).

How can we rejoice in the light of those words? They remind us that the ageing experience is part of God's curse (Genesis 3:17-19; Romans 5:12) for sin coming into the world, and continuing to corrupt the human race. That is true, but as Christians we have the glorious New Testament certainty of the new heaven and the new earth (2 Peter 3:13). This hope is a bright light in a dark place and that light shines on us. I have seen elderly people poring over newspapers in horror and watching the television news saying 'what is the world coming to — where will it all end?' Let us look beyond and above these things to the Lord of glory. These words from Psalm 90 also remind us of our personal sins, even our secret sins. But, here again, we have the assurance that God has pardoned our sins through the Lord Jesus Christ. In him God says to us 'their sins and lawless acts I will remember no more' (Hebrews 10:17).

It is foolish to suggest that we can ignore the increasing effects of old age upon us. Nor can we forget the state of the world around us or the sins that still haunt us. But these must not be allowed to be the whole story, nor even the major part of the story. The great thing is to rejoice in the Lord. We must think about him, his greatness and glory and the wonder of his grace in our lives. He is always worthy of our praise and our delight.

You may be house-bound because of your age or ill-health, and you feel useless and even forgotten. A pastor recently told me that when he visited people in that situation, he encouraged them to look back. He did not mean that they should wish their younger days could return, nor did he mean that they should dwell on the bad times or on their sins and failures. He meant that they should recall what the Lord had done for them in the past despite their weaknesses and shortcomings. Why not try to take his advice?

I'm sure that this pastor did not limit his advice to remembering God's goodness in the past. The backward look is helpful but so is the upward look. Psalm 29 gives us a graphic picture of a thunderstorm. You can see the lightning and feel the power of the tempest, and then comes the wonderful affirmation

> 'The LORD sits enthroned over the flood; the LORD is enthroned as king for ever. The LORD gives strength to his people; the LORD blesses his people with peace' (Psalm 29:10, 11).

God is in control of what is happening to you, nothing is out of hand, nor can it be. So rejoice!

And then there is the onward look. This is perhaps the greatest reason of all to sing —

We expect a bright tomorrow,
All will be well;
Faith can sing, through days of sorrow,
All, all is well:
On our Father's love relying,
Jesus every need supplying,
Or in living or in dying,
All must be well.

(Mary Peters, 1813-56)

How does this work out in practice? This is what we will be exploring in the following pages — so stay with us.

There are some situations that perhaps test our rejoicing more than others. One of these is where we brought up children and did our best to lead them to faith in Jesus Christ, but now we're nearing the end of our days and those children are unconverted, or even possibly reject the Lord. It is natural that questions arise in our minds as to where we went wrong; could we have done better? We may be able to see clearly the mistakes we made. But such thoughts must not be allowed to quench our joy in the Lord. Remember that salvation is always of the Lord and is always despite our failings. No parents are ever perfect in the handling of their children, some are even converted despite having unconverted, ungodly parents! Continue to love them and pray for them and then leave the rest with the Lord.

It is unreasonable and unnatural for us to try to prove our joy in the Lord by constantly laughing or repeatedly saying 'praise the Lord'. We will never convince ourselves or others in this way that our joy in the Lord is genuine. Nehemiah said 'the joy of the LORD is your strength' (Nehemiah 8:10). What God gives we don't need to manufacture!

CHAPTER THREE

Growing Old Graciously

There were two sisters who were in their nineties when I first met them. Until recently they had walked six miles over the hilly fields to church every Sunday. Their garden frightened me because of its size and its weedless orderliness and productivity. It was harvest thanksgiving time so we put some fruit in a little attractive package as a small love gift to our two friends among others. The older sister, bless her heart, was most offended. They didn't need such charity; they could look after themselves; what was intended as an act of affection was seen as an insult, and it took the gentle persuasion of the younger sister to achieve a reluctant willingness to receive the fruit.

It is not always easy to receive gifts we do not need, or that we do not want to admit that we need, but how else can our friends express their love and affection for us? If we resent their gifts we are stifling one of the most precious things in life, friendship, and as we grow older we need friends more than ever, whether we like it or not!

Even if we do need help and the gifts offered us are very appropriate, there is sometimes a feeling of resentment that we are seen to be needy people. This is especially so if, in earlier days, we have been the ones to help others and to give generously. Whatever our situation, one of the signs of growing old graciously is knowing how to receive gifts or help of any kind with true gratitude and appreciation for the thoughts, intentions and affection of the givers.

David, the Psalmist, paints a lovely picture. It is of an eastern home with a courtyard at its centre and in the middle of the courtyard there is a palm tree, old and gnarled. It has been there probably as long as any of the family can remember; all down the years it has never failed to yield its fruit and even now, as the seasons pass, it never becomes useless or prompts the thought that it should be cut down. David says,

> 'the righteous will flourish like a palm tree ... they will still bear fruit in old age, they will stay fresh and green' (Psalm 92: 12,14).[1]

In chapter 14 we will think a little more about prayer, but let us remind ourselves here that the roots of that tree needed to go deeply down for moisture and nourishment. Likewise, there is every good reason for elderly people not to let up on prayer and meditation on the Scriptures, because this is the only way to keep spiritually fresh and to 'bear fruit in old age'.

When I retired, I asked myself a lot of questions. What would I do with my remaining years? What would I do if I became housebound, bedridden or even totally dependent on others to do everything for me? What would the Lord's purpose be for me in those circumstances? I came to the conclusion that there is one purpose in life that never goes away and is with us to the end in every situation, without exception. That one thing was the requirement to be Christlike. As Paul put it

> 'And we know that in all things God works for the good of those who love him, who have been called according to his purpose. For those God foreknew he also predestined to be conformed to the likeness of his son ... '(Romans 8: 28-29).

I became so sure of this that I began to explore the character of Jesus that I was meant to strive for. As a result, I wrote a book called *The Beauty of Jesus* to remind me that the great privilege of reflecting him is never taken from us. Some elderly people can testify that the Lord has used them in bringing about the conversion of others to Jesus Christ. We should certainly use every opportunity to bear our Christian witness and this is always a great joy, but such opportunities come and go, while the challenge to be Christ-like never leaves us. Let us remember, that there is a very close connection between witnessing and Christlikeness. We are very unlikely to recommend our Lord to other people if our lives do not remind them of him. But even when we're alone our thoughts, attitudes and habits can be Christ-like and, like hidden flowers in the wild, glorify God even when no other eye sees us but his.

Too often, older people are prone to bitterness, a critical spirit, ingratitude and irritability. A study by a psychologist has recently concluded that cantankerous people live longer than others. With due respect, we prefer the Scripture that says

> ' … in quietness and trust is your strength' (Isaiah 30:15).

Some people are blessed with lives longer than most others. Such blessing is tempered as they see their brothers, sisters or friends they have known for many years, leaving them one by one until they alone are left. This can easily give rise to a sense of lonely bitterness and is a big test of their joy in the Lord. If you feel like that, try to remember the perfection of the Lord's timing. Try to be pleased that those you grieve about are enjoying heaven's glory, and to accept that the Lord has left you behind to live for him, no matter what your circumstances might be.

There is an old English proverb 'the older the fiddle the sweeter the tune'. By God's grace, this can be true for all of us who are God's people. This is in complete contrast to the non-Christian view that says with Matthew Arnold ' … and a sigh that one thing only has been lent to youth and age in common — discontent'.

We began with just one example of bearing fruit in old age, the grace of receiving gifts. Our Lord had need of nothing but yet graciously received the hospitality of Martha and Mary and begged water from a Samaritan woman. Thankfulness is important — with a smile of course.

This seventeenth century prayer touches well on a number of other things that challenge us: -

17th Century Nun's Prayer

LORD Thou knowest better than I know myself that I am growing older and will some day be old.
Keep me from the fatal habit of thinking I must say something on every subject and on every occasion.
Release me from craving to straighten out everybody's affairs.
Make me thoughtful but not moody; helpful but not bossy. With my vast store of wisdom it seems a pity not to use it all, but Thou Lord knowest that I want a few friends at the end.
Keep my mind free from the recital of endless details; give me wings to get to the point.
Seal my lips on my aches and pains. They are increasing and love of rehearsing them is becoming sweeter as the years go by. I dare not ask for grace enough to enjoy the tales of other's pains, but help me to endure them with patience. I dare not ask for an improved memory, but for a growing humility and a lessening cocksureness when my memory seems to clash with the memories of others. Teach me the glorious lesson that occasionally I may be mistaken.
Keep me reasonably sweet; I do not want to be a Saint — some of them are so hard to live with — but a sour old person is one of the crowning works of the devil.
Give me the ability to see good things in unexpected places and talents in unexpected people.
And give me, O LORD, the grace to tell them so. Amen.

There is something ugly and repelling about a senior citizen who is bitter, critical or complaining; but one who is thankful, understanding and appreciative is a great blessing. Don Carson perfectly describes people like this: '… their physical strength is reduced, nevertheless they become more and more steadfast and radiant. Their memories may be fading; their arthritis may be nearly unbearable; their ventures beyond their small rooms or apartments may be severely curtailed. But somehow they live as if they already have one foot in heaven.'

---

[1] See Spurgeon on Psalm 92:13 in '*The Treasury of David*'.

CHAPTER FOUR

God's Promises

The Old Testament prophets were always pouring scorn on the idols worshipped by the heathen and hankered after by the people of Israel. One of those prophets was Isaiah and he ridiculed the idols because, just when people wanted help, they themselves had to be carried. Instead of helping those who were weak, the weak had the additional burden of carrying their idols!

> 'The images that are carried about are burdensome, a burden for the weary' (Isaiah 46:1).

Now, after what has been said in the first three chapters, you may feel that all I have done is to add to your burdens. The challenge is to accept old age, to be gracious and Christlike — oh dear! These challenges could be as burdensome as the idols that had to be carried, except for one thing, God's promises. When we take these to heart, the weight is lifted. Isaiah's purpose was to contrast the idols with Israel's God and ours, and the promises he made. God said:

> 'Listen to me, O house of Jacob, all you who remain of the house of Israel, you whom I have upheld since you were conceived, and have carried since your birth. Even to your old age and grey hairs I am he, I am he who will sustain you. I have made you and I will carry you; I will sustain you and I will rescue you' (Isaiah 46:3-4).

Our God does not lay on us impossible burdens, nor does he have to be carried, he carries us!

There is an old song, 'standing on the promises of God my Saviour'. This is right, we need to believe what God has promised to do for us, but perhaps we should go further and realise that what this means is relying on the God who made the promises. Isaiah shows us just how tender, how patient, how understanding and how faithful our God is.

One of the older hymns begins 'How firm a foundation, ye saints of the Lord, is laid for your faith in his excellent word!' In a later verse the writer turns the text from Isaiah 46 into verse:

E'en down to old age all my people shall prove
My sovereign, eternal, unchangeable love;
And when hoary hairs shall their temples adorn,
Like lambs they shall still in my bosom be borne.

Maybe, with all your aches and pains and problems that will not go away, you feel like a martyr. If so, then remember, as I said before, that the God who gave the martyrs the strength to remain true to the Lord, despite all the terrible treatment they received, is your God too. Take some inspiration from one of the earliest to suffer for Christ's sake, a man named Polycarp. When he was challenged to deny the Lord he said — 'eighty and six years have I served him, and he has done me no wrong. How then can I blaspheme my King and my Saviour?'

Another promise that applies to people like us is the one given by God to the tribe of Asher —

' ... your strength will equal your days' (Deuteronomy 33:25).

This does not limit the promise to certain conditions or even certain ages. No matter what state we're in, so long as we are alive in this world, the Lord has undertaken to give us the strength we need to bear the physical stresses and to live in a way that pleases him. As the apostle Paul discovered ' ... when I am weak, then I am strong' (2 Corinthians 12:10).

I wonder if you have been falling into the trap of living as though the older we grow, the promises of God are less real to us; they diminish in significance as we diminish in strength. Let us get this fixed into our minds and memories, that all God's promises are valid throughout our lives, to the very end. Here is a selection for you to test just how firmly you still hold on to them.

> 'I will instruct you and teach you in the way you should go; I will counsel you and watch over you' (Psalm 32:8).
>
> 'You will keep in perfect peace him whose mind is steadfast, because he trusts in you' (Isaiah 26:3).
>
> 'But now, this is what the LORD says — he who created you O Jacob, he who formed you, O Israel: "Fear not, for I have redeemed you; I have summoned you by name; you are mine. When you pass through the waters, I will be with you; and when you pass through the rivers, they will not sweep over you"' (Isaiah 43: 1-2).
>
> 'For my Father's will is that everyone who looks to the Son and believes in him shall have eternal life, and I will raise him up at the last day' (John 6:40).
>
> 'My sheep listen to my voice; I know them, and they follow me. I give them eternal life, and they shall never perish; no one can snatch them out of my hand. My Father, who has given them to me, is greater than all; no one can snatch them out of my Father's hand' (John 10:27-29).
>
> ' ... being confident of this, that he who began a good work in you will carry it on to completion until the day of Christ Jesus' (Philippians 1:6).
>
> 'And my God will meet all your needs according to his glorious riches in Christ Jesus' (Philippians 4:19).
>
> ' ... God has said, "never will I leave you; never will I forsake you"' (Hebrews 13:5).

The poet Robert Southey, who in later life was Poet Laureate, celebrated the faithfulness of God in verses that reflect Ecclesiastes 12:1 in a poem entitled 'The Old Man's Comforts and how he gained them'.

You are old, Father William, the young man cried,
The few locks which are left you are grey;
You are hale, Father William, a hearty old man,
Now tell me the reason, I pray.

In the days of my youth, Father William replied,
I remember'd that youth would fly fast,
And abused not my health and my vigour at first,
That I never might need them at last.

You are old, Father William, the young man cried,
And pleasure with youth pass away;
And yet you lament not the days that are gone,
Now tell me the reason, I pray.

In the days of my youth, Father William replied,
I remember'd that youth could not last;
I thought of the future, whatever I did,
That I never might grieve for the past.

You are old, Father William, the young man cried,
And life must be hastening away;
You are cheerful, and love to converse upon death,
Now tell me the reason, I pray.

I am, cheerful, young man, Father William replied,
Let the cause thy attention engage;
In the days of my youth I remember'd my God!
And He hath not forgotten my age.

Even if you were not committed to the Lord in earlier years or have only lately come to faith in Christ, the promises still apply to you. There is no waiting time; the moment you trust in Jesus Christ, all the promises of God are yours.

So let us put both feet down on God's promises. He is the living God and will not fail to honour every one of his undertakings for his people.

CHAPTER FIVE

Antiques Are Valuable!

Antiques are valuable, even if they lie in some dusty corner only to be remembered when they have to be moved for their space to be used for some other purpose! Perhaps you feel like an antique, belonging to another world and taking up useful space in the present one; but I want to convince you that, nevertheless, you are valuable and you need to believe it!

So you're feeling sorry for yourself because age is taking its toll on your strength and you are increasingly limited in what you can do! Very well — here is a question for you, 'do you realise that you are a blessing to society?' You may say 'that is a silly question, how can I be a blessing to the community when I cost the Health Service a fortune on drugs and ointments; when I am one of an increasing number of senior citizens who make more and more demands on the Welfare State? People like me are no good to anyone, we're a terrible drain on society.'

I understand what you say especially if you are becoming more and more dependent on others to help you with the shopping, the housework or looking after yourself. As you gradually lose your independence, your privacy and your ability to order your life as you used to do, you are also in danger of losing your self respect and self-esteem.

And then, maybe, you have been made to feel like that because you have been treated as a nuisance by some callous official, or even by your own family, when they ought to know better. You really must be careful of thinking like this. For one thing it seems you are forgetting that God intends to be a blessing to you just as you are, and to make you a blessing to others, as we shall see. But perhaps even more seriously, such thinking has led some people to consider asking for their lives to be ended and they have even been tempted to hasten the process. We will consider this in more detail in chapter 23, but for now make up your mind that such ideas are not for the Christian.

God says you are a blessing to society. As David Gay reminds us, 'in the world of nature, autumn is the time for falling leaves. But that season is, in some respects, the most glorious of the entire year.'

When God wanted to give us a picture of a perfect city, prosperous, joyful and at peace, this is what he said —

> 'Once again men and women of ripe old age, will sit in the streets of Jerusalem, each with cane in hand because of his age' (Zechariah 8:4).

So let us think about some of the ways in which you and I are essential to a healthy society. This doesn't mean that we can become proud and make a nuisance of ourselves by making unreasonable demands on others. But it does mean that we should not allow ourselves to feel we have no useful place in society, or that the sooner we are out of the way, the better for all.

Let us challenge such thinking for what it is! It is thinking without God, as though God has not loved us and has no further use for us. It is the way ungodly people speak — 'old age is a shipwreck' (Marshall Petain) — 'age I do abhor thee, youth I do adore thee' (Shakespeare in the 'Passionate Pilgrim').

Our ideas should always be shaped by what God says in the Bible. Contrary to our secular society, which often sees older people as a liability, the Bible regards them as a blessing, for example

> 'Walk in all the way that the LORD your God has commanded you, so that you may live and prosper and prolong your days in the land that you will possess' (Deuteronomy 5:33).

> 'Never again will there be in it (Jerusalem) an infant that lives but a few days, or an old man who does not live out his years; he who dies at a hundred will be thought a mere youth; he who fails to reach a hundred will be considered accursed' (Isaiah 65:20).

Robert Browning caught the attitude to ageing that arises from such texts —

> 'Grow old along with me! The best is yet to be,
> The last of life, for which the first was made.'

In other words, all our previous years have been a preparation for the Lord's blessing in our later years. That is a complete reversal of the thinking of people who have no faith in God. As one 80 year old single lady puts it, she lives 'counting each day as a bonus since I retired'.

Some years ago I was a youthful leader of a young people's holiday house party and I was followed the next week by a much older man. I have to confess to some feeling of hurt when one of my own youth group expressed appreciation of him but made no comment about me! This taught me that older people, who have the right attitudes can be a blessing to those who are younger in a way that their peers cannot be. Just recently my fellow elder, over seventy years old, gave his testimony at an evening service. It was one of the younger members who told me very cheerfully, how much she had appreciated what he had said and how helpful it had been.

None of this should surprise us since long ago the writer of Psalm 71 gave his testimony like this —

> 'Since my youth, O God, you have taught me, and to this day I declare your marvellous deeds. Even when I am old and grey, do not forsake me, O God, till I declare your power to the next generation, your might to all who are to come' (Psalm 71:17-18).

Now you may be saying 'but those people were active, I am housebound, inactive and useless'. As you will see as we proceed in this book, it is our contention that even in that condition the Lord is able to bless us and to make us a blessing.

'Growing older is liberating. As we age we enter what psychologist Carl Jung called "the second half of life" and it's the better half because we don't have to prove anything any more. We know who we are. We've discovered what works in our life and what doesn't. We have experienced the goodness of God in depths and dimensions that younger people haven't yet found. We can talk about those, live them, demonstrate them.' (Roger Palms)

A couple who have had their ruby wedding and then perhaps their golden wedding anniversary may feel that they are useless now. Little do they know that young people contemplating marriage, need the encouragement that comes from the sight of people whose love has endured for forty or fifty years and more. All that couple have to do is to go on loving each other and they are a blessing.

Or, here is a single Christian lady now retired. Many years ago she refused the offer of marriage from a man who was not a Christian. She remained single throughout the years that have followed and she has lived life to the full despite the fact that she now also cares for her aged mother. She is still the most cheerful, fulfilled person you could wish to meet. What a tremendous help her example is today to any Christian girl who is tempted to marry a non-Christian man, fearing the consequences of a single life! What a blessing she is in her later years proving what the Lord is able to do for those who honour him!

What would society be like without people like us to provide and care for? It would become hard, callous and self centred! So you see, it is a blessing to a nation to learn how to deal in compassion, tenderness and generosity with its ageing population.

With the Lord's help, our lives can be a blessing to others, even in advancing years. There is a strange verse in the book of Proverbs,

> 'the fruit of righteousness is a tree of life' (Proverbs 11:30).

This means that our lives can grow in usefulness as the years go by; it has a similar meaning to the Lord's invitation

> 'If any one is thirsty let him come to me and drink. Whoever believes in me, as the Scripture has said, streams of living water will flow from within him' (John 7:37-38).

As we grow older, in one sense we become the ones in need — the thirsty ones. But Jesus says he can make us into people from whose lives the needs of others are met. What a transformation! We infirm, creaky-jointed oldies become useful to others by what we are and what we say, and by attitude to life, quite apart from what we may or may not be able to do.

'Every person is equal in God's sight — irrespective of age. In the body of Christ, the parts that the world think are less honourable, the vulnerable and infirm — we must treat "with special honour" (1 Corinthians 12: 12-31).' (CARE Action File)

CHAPTER SIX

Just Testing!

Paddy had been in a good way of business, as anyone experiencing the quality of his home had no need to be told. Now he had reached retirement age and looked forward to enjoying the benefit of his well earned resources. Like the good business man he was, he reckoned that this was the right time to take stock, only now it was not a case of reviewing the state of the firm and the prospect of future profits. Paddy began to take stock of his life and especially to assess how best he could face the challenge of advancing years. His father had been a Methodist preacher and now, after years of neglect, Paddy recalled some of the things he had heard as a child. His conclusion was that he must 'get this religious thing' sorted out.

Perhaps you are about to retire, or you may have already done so, and you have had all kinds of decisions to make. What makes those decisions difficult is the obvious fact that you do not know how long you are going to live. I am sorry to be so blunt, but I don't think this book will be very helpful to you unless together we face our situation honestly and frankly and without too much 'beating about the bush'.

You know that it makes sense to be clear about your eternal destiny. Many people, all their lives, deceive themselves that they will be more willing to consider such things when they are older, but it is a fact that this is a delusion. People are no more willing at 65 to think about life after death than they were at 25. Not only so, their minds are now more set in their own opinions, and soon the time comes when they are not able to think clearly and then — time gone! This verse, found on a clock in Chester Cathedral, is worth considering —

When, as a child, I laughed and wept,
Time crept,
When, as a youth, I waxed more bold,
Time strolled.
When I became a full-grown man,
Time ran.
When older still I daily grew,
Time flew.
Soon I shall find, in passing on,
Time gone.
O Christ, wilt thou have saved me then?
Amen.

Canon Henry Twells, 1823 – 1900

So it is not surprising that in the Bible we are taught to pray that God will

> 'teach us to number our days aright, that we may gain a heart of wisdom' (Psalm 90:12),

and it is wisdom to be sure that we are ready for the life to come. This means we need to be sure that we are right with God.

One of the people we read about in the Bible is a man called Enoch. We are told that when he reached the age of 65, he began to 'walk with God' (Genesis 5:21-24) which means that he began to live with God! Let us work out how his experience can be real for us. Paddy, whom we met at the beginning of this chapter, decided that the best thing he could do was to go to a church, but the first one to which he went did not seem to speak to him at all. The teaching wasn't anything like what he remembered from his father. At last he found a place where the preaching was firmly based on the Bible and the people were taught how to be reconciled to God through Jesus Christ, so at last, Paddy committed himself to Jesus Christ and began his life with God. Another elderly man has spoken of his experience; 'my advice to younger people is to get with Jesus as soon as possible … when I think of the wasted years that I have had, I could weep'. An aged married couple agreed that 'a person who is not a Christian is living in darkness and our Lord is the light, and if you have the Lord in your life, things are so much better, and you face things so much better.'

If you are not attending a church like the one Paddy found, an evangelical church, then why not make that your first move? As you ask the Lord to help you, the rest will follow. The life with God begins with his pardon as we trust in Jesus Christ and all he has done for us in his life, death and resurrection, and it does not end, because he promises to be with us all the time, right through death itself and on to eternal glory. He has promised that he will never leave you (Hebrews 13:5).

I don't know how old the jailer in Philippi was when he was converted, but he was certainly no youngster. He asked Paul and Silas, 'Sirs, what must I do to be saved?' Think carefully about

> their answer and do something about it now! They said, 'Believe in the Lord Jesus, and you will be saved …'

(Acts 16: 30-31).

The rest of this book is really about how this life with God works out as we grow older. Now is the time, especially if you have not thought about it before, to think your way into the later years of your life. Without God, age becomes a meaningless burden, a road with no light in the tunnel or at the end of it. With God we can speak of the blessings and positive benefits of old age. One of my friends remembers hearing a sermon when he was 14 years old on 'the devil has no happy old men'. People who are not Christians are in Satan's domain and he will see to it that their old age will be beset by fear and frustration. When we are Christians, God does not take away the effects of age on our bodies or our minds, but he does make them bearable. The Lord gives peace and joy and meaning to life, even into old age. In the process he makes us useful and at the end of it all, everlasting glory awaits us.

CHAPTER SEVEN

Relax!

Very often people say to me 'Christians never retire, do they?' Now I try to be polite and exercise a degree of Christian courtesy, so I tend to smile sympathetically and change the subject. Actually, what I feel like doing is to say rather firmly 'of course Christians retire, and it is a great pity if they cannot or will not do so, or are not allowed to do so.' There are earnest Christians who genuinely think that the whole idea of retirement is wrong. If they mean that our obligation to live godly and Christlike lives does not end until we reach the conclusion of our days on earth, then we are very happy to agree with them. In fact, that is the main theme of this book. Again, if they mean that we should never tire of playing our part in making the gospel of Jesus Christ known to others in our locality and throughout the world, we wholeheartedly agree as will become evident in the following chapters.

But if we think there is something wrong in easing off from the tensions and burdens we have lived with during our working years, then we are robbing ourselves of many new blessings, and we are doing so without good reason. So relax, but that does not mean you should just vegetate; there is no joy in doing nothing! Try to set yourself some objectives that keep you alert and alive. You need to make sure that your objectives are achievable or else you will soon give up in frustration. What does the Lord want you to do? Ask him, and think it out.

Sometimes there are circumstances such as ill-health, that take the shine off the benefits of retirement and make it less enjoyable. But what a blessing it is when the pressures of paid employment are lifted! What a joy now to spend more time with a partner or friends, to stay in bed a little longer, have an after dinner nap (if you like that sort of thing!) or to develop an interest or hobby that has been, perforce, neglected until now. God has given us more interests, more skills and appreciations than can possibly be fulfilled until we are relieved of the 'work for a living' routine. This leaves entirely out of account new time for prayer, Bible study and Christian fellowship. I am not denying that our paid employment was our vocation, in which God intended us to glorify him, but I am saying that there is a vocation of senior citizenship in which God calls us to live for him and enjoy his blessings no less than before.

So, now is the time to relax. This is good for us mentally because retired people should be less tense than in earlier times and have a greater sense of well-being. This is good also for their family relationships; how often a woman who has been a housewife for many years, has looked forward to the companionship of the man she loves when he retires, only to be disappointed because he has not relaxed or come to terms with his new situation.

Oh! I know that wives sometimes complain 'I don't know what to do with him, he is under my feet all day!' But they don't really mean it! Alas, at times, a closer relationship can be disastrous because of a lack of love in the first place, but normally we should welcome the opportunity now to do things together, no matter whether it is housework, walking or something else of common interest.

It is true that there is not much about this in the Bible to guide us, but let us notice one interesting example where God commanded men to retire (Numbers 8:23-26). The Levites looked after the tent for worship by the Israelites, while they travelled on their way to the promised land. When these Levites reached the age of 50 (!!) they were told they must retire —

> 'but at the age of fifty, they must retire from their regular service and work no longer' (Numbers 8:25).

We will notice in our next chapter what they were allowed to do and what some of them actually did in retirement, but for the moment, let us simply notice that they were relieved of the responsibility of the demands of heavy work. Such is God's compassion; we do not serve a harsh slave-driving master, and for many people the sheer relief of no longer bearing responsibility is what retirement means.

Perhaps this is the place to sound a note of warning. It is all too easy to waste our time when the pressures of enforced daily routine are off. The result will be that we become bored, and such a life is neither pleasing to the Lord nor helpful to others. There is a special danger if we are not naturally disciplined or orderly people. The secret is to have some kind of structure in mind that is not so rigid as to be a burden and yet clear enough to ensure that we actually get things done. For example, in our home we use mornings for work in the house and such things as writing books! Then we set aside certain days for different activities.

When I was working with the Grace Baptist Mission and my grey hairs indicated that I was nearing retirement, I noticed that often, when hymns were chosen at meetings where I was speaking, the one just before my part, had in it the verse —

His work my hoary age shall bless
When youthful vigour is no more;
And my last hour of life confess
His love hath animating power.

I'm not sure if the choice was a deliberate comment on my age, but when you come to think about it, that is a very good resolve, is it not?

CHAPTER EIGHT

Busier Than Ever?

I once heard about a man whose idea of retirement was that it was an opportunity to do nothing! From the first day of his release from work, he sat in a chair in front of his television and didn't move day after day. He expected his wife to wait on him with his meals while he lazed and slept his time away. That must be very rare, but when it happens it is thoroughly miserable for everyone else, and much worse, it is grievously dishonouring to the Lord.

But then, not long ago, I was at a conference where one of the themes was about the way Christians face retirement. One of the pastors said 'I need some help. I have a retired man in the church whom I cannot stop working. He just doesn't give up. How can I prevent him working himself to death?' The man just wouldn't trust his business to others, and so well after retirement age, he was starting at 4 a.m. each day and carrying on as he had done before. Not surprisingly, he had a heart attack and other problems, but these made no difference. To say the least, this is eccentric and it surely betrays a lack of thought about the best way to use the opportunity of retirement. These two examples give me great sympathy with another pastor, who for other reasons exclaimed one day, 'oh, that the Lord would send me normal people'!

'What will you do when you retire?' The question is frequently asked and there are plenty of people ready and willing to offer advice. The answer will vary very much from person to person. We reach retirement age in different stages of health which will affect how we spend our time. We all have different abilities, skills and talents and a variety of home and family situations will shape our thinking. Nevertheless, there are some biblical principles that Christians will have in mind as they consider retirement.

Before we go any further, I want to mention Henry. He was made redundant many years before he reached the retirement age of 65. Now Henry did not have many talents, nor was he highly educated, so what did he do? The answer is that before long, just about every housebound or handicapped person in his village and further afield, came to rely on him for their shopping and odd jobs. Everyone knew about Henry and many were thankful for him and his bicycle.

This book is mainly for people who are reaching the later stages of life, but I am aware of an increasing number who, like Henry, find themselves in retirement long before retirement age and are still fit mentally and physically. This period of early retirement is called The *Bonus Years* in a book of that title by John Cansdale, published in 1979. Some people have been made redundant and cannot find work, others retire voluntarily. Reactions to this vary considerably. It may be bitterness, frustration or bewilderment, or it could be a positive approach, like Henry's with his bicycle. The Christian response must surely be to ask the Lord for guidance into a useful way of life for his glory.

Some people have given way to the temptation to spend their time in a spate of leisure with selfish pursuits for amusement. Others might descend to an orgy of self-pity, especially if they have been unfairly treated. Those who believe that God is in control of all things, will apply that belief to this situation and find out why the Lord has given them so much spare time. Churches, missions and charities must benefit from this development in our society as an increasing number of skills of all kinds become freely or, possibly, cheaply available. Let us learn from the man who at an early age had earned enough money to live on for the rest of his life. Instead of piling up more and more wealth, he retired in order to spend all his time helping other people.

But now, let us consider how those who retire at 65 should

approach that prospect. Friends and relatives will advise them to take up new and exciting hobbies to occupy their minds and hands. It is a good idea, but all too often, it blots out other important possibilities. I wonder how often people, about to retire, go to their church leaders asking if there is anything they can do to help the church?

In chapter 7 we referred to the Levites who had to retire at the age of 50. But that was not the end of the story, because the law went on to say

> 'They may assist their brothers in performing their duties ... ' (Numbers 8:26).

Not only so, but some of them developed a gift of writing poetry resulting in some of the Psalms, such as Psalms 73-85. It would surprise me greatly if nothing could be found for you to do in your local church. It could be visiting, cleaning, duplicating, secretarial work, or building repairs. When Harold Spratt retired, he seemed to live on the church premises, there was always a repair job to do. Georgie made refreshments for the mothers and toddlers group and was an official visitor at a Pilgrim Home. The list is endless, and there will probably be time for a hobby as well.

Many ladies, whose main occupation has been maintaining the home, will want to say; 'It's all right for you men, what about us? We can't retire. The house still has to be cleaned and the meals provided!' Situations differ, but generally it must be sensible and right for these duties to be shared. For very good reasons, I am not expected to be involved in the cooking! But, dusting, hoovering, washing-up and gardening are my regular chores! Retirement is an opportunity to work together and enjoy a partner's company in a way not normally possible before. Love can be expressed in all kinds of practical ways.

For those who live alone, life tends to go on much the same, but after retirement, they too, have more time to serve the Lord in the church and in helping others.

When people say to me 'you are just as busy as ever', I know that they are being deceived. Unless we are very silly, as we grow older we do not work at the same speed or under the same constant pressure as before; we only appear to be busier, but really that is an illusion. The important thing is to pace ourselves. There is no sense in ignoring the fact that we're not as young as we used to be, so we will ease off the pace, but not so much as to be lazy. It is not kind to our loved ones if we risk heart trouble and other problems through lack of carefulness, nor is there any joy in being idle.

Evangeline Cory Booth was surely right when she said 'it is not how many years we live, but what we do with them.' In chapter 7, we urged that retirement is the opportunity to relax the tensions of past years. This must include the mind and the body, but both mind and body need to be exercised. Now is the time to read books we have been too busy to open. We must keep our minds active about the society in which we live, and we now have the opportunity to explore the rich variety of Christian literature all around us. We need physical exercise to keep healthy. I tend to dislike walking, so it is a good thing my paper shop is far enough away to ensure a regular walk each morning. It is just at this point that we can fall into a trap. We can spend so much time exercising mind and body for our own sakes, that we have no time left for some kind of work for the Lord and support for the various activities of the church.

So let us sit down, with our partner if possible, and think through what we plan to do. Let us ask the advice of a church leader to help us to work out how our talents can still be used for the Lord or find new ways of serving him.

CHAPTER NINE

A Fight To Be Fought

It was her ninetieth birthday and she was asked to choose a chorus at the Women's Meeting. What did she choose? As the speaker that day, I was first amused, but then thrilled as we all sang her choice, it was:

> There's a fight to be fought and a race to be won,
> There are dangers to meet by the way.

A fight to be fought at ninety years old? Yes indeed; that lady knew the reality and she was honest about it.

It is true that some temptations diminish or even disappear altogether with age, but it is also true that others intensify whilst new ones seem to emerge from nowhere. The fact is that the devil does not stop trying to trip us up and to destroy us right to the end, so there are always dangers to meet, both physical and spiritual. A retired pastor says 'Earnest attention should be given to fighting the good fight of faith, to maintain Christian life and experience. The spiritual warfare may change somewhat with age, but it does not cease'.

We all expect our physical powers to lose their strength as we grow older, so it may surprise us that sexual desire can stay with us with enough strength to get us into trouble. If you doubt that, do not forget that King David was by no means a young man when he lusted after the beautiful Bathsheba, and of his son King Solomon we read,

> 'King Solomon, however, loved many foreign women ... As Solomon grew old, his wives turned his heart after other gods, and his heart was not fully devoted to the LORD his God' (1 Kings 11: 1-6).

Sadly, our newspapers continue with the evidence.

All too often, even Christian people are divorcing in their later years because a new fascination has overtaken them. A beautiful woman or a charming man may rightly excite our admiration, but there is a short step from admiration to lustful desire unless we maintain a firm control on our minds and our imaginations. As always, Satan attacks us when we are most vulnerable, so it is at a time of illness or some other test of our love, that some new attraction comes on the scene. Since we are Christians, young people have a right to expect better of us, and they look for us to be good examples of maturity and godliness. Even in old age, our sins do not merely degrade us, they dishonour our Lord and disappoint those who look for the evidence in us of God's enabling grace.

At the spiritual level, perhaps one of the most common sins into which we fall is that of jealousy. There was once a popular Convention speaker named F. B. Meyer. His popularity held sway for many years until, as he grew older, the star of a younger man, Campbell Morgan, rose and gradually displaced him. What an opportunity for jealousy! But it was said at that time that never had Meyer's godliness and humility shone brighter than as he gradually receded into the background and the talk was all of the young Morgan.

How often jealousy has embittered Christian preachers and other workers as other younger or more gifted people have come along to replace them! This is a touchy subject, but it is also a common pastoral problem. For example, when should this ageing organist, Bible class leader, women's fellowship president step down? On the one hand, there are sins of arrogance and impatience in younger people to be dealt with, and the honour of Christ is at stake in what is done and the way it is done.

But, on the other hand, we older people need to watch ourselves. It is wrong to hinder the work by holding on to jobs when we know we are 'past it', but it is equally wrong to give up when we could easily carry on, leaving a gap nobody is available to fill. The grace we need is to be honest with ourselves, with our fellow-workers and our leaders. We need humility to continue or to step down, whichever is right, with good grace. That is not easy, but grace comes from the Lord, so ask him for it. (We will say a little more about this in chapter 13).

Another spiritual temptation is to become cool about the Lord and his work. Roger Palms compels us to ask ourselves some searching questions, 'Am I on board with what God is doing now, to-day? The fields of God will have a harvest; will I be part of it? Was I part of yesterday's blaze but to-day's cold ember? If I've dropped out of the fire, should I be praying, God throw me back in and let me burn well?'

Older people sometimes give expression to very wrong thoughts, like 'I've done my bit over the years, now I'm retired, let the younger ones get on with it. I'm out of it now; it's up to them.' It is one thing to be willing graciously to step down from the 'front line' at the right time, but it is quite another to wash our hands of the work we once lived for. We must beware of the temptation to lose interest just because we are no longer active in the work. It is important still to be willing to give advice when it is asked for, or to lend a hand, if we can, when the need arises. People who take over from us should be assured of our continuing prayers, understanding and support.

There is also the temptation to succumb to what we might call 'withdrawal symptoms'. This is the danger of becoming depressed because we are no longer at the centre of things in the church. We feel a kind of emptiness, because active work in the church once filled our lives. This can be very distressing. We may not be aware of what is happening to us; all we know is that we have these feelings of emptiness or even of rejection, and we should ask the Lord to help us to cope with them.

Another big temptation for ageing people is to develop an

unforgiving spirit. We can get into the habit of looking back and brooding over things we think other people have done to us in the past, all the unkind things that have been said and all the thanks we should have received but were not forthcoming. This not only poisons relationships with a whole lot of people, but it produces a heart of malice and bitterness that affects our whole life. Forgiveness is a great healer and is as good for the forgiver as for the forgiven. Paul wrote

> 'love ... keeps no record of wrongs' (1 Corinthians 13:5),

and if we have difficulty in forgiving people who have offended us and in forgetting their supposed wrong, we should remember that when we have Jesus Christ as our Lord and Saviour, God's undertaking to us is

> 'their sins and lawless acts I will remember no more' (Hebrews 10:17).

Since we have received such undeserved mercy, we should surely have the same merciful attitude.

So we see that older people must not slacken in their watch over their spiritual state; as David Gay says 'A fine testimony of a Christian can easily be marred in old age,' and it is certain that the evil one would be very delighted this should happen. Let us not be like king Asa of Judah who began well and

> 'did what was good and right in the eyes of the LORD' (2 Chronicles 14:2),

but 'ended his days rebellious against God's will ... a grumbling old man, instead of a humble servant longing to see his master'! (*Geneva Bible Notes* on 2 Chronicles 16 on 16th December 2000)

CHAPTER TEN

'A' Level At 70 Plus

You might have thought that examinations were only for children and young people, if so you are in for a surprise! The Bible challenges us with something we did not expect; it requires us to sit a test for those of advanced years! You will find your 'A' level paper in Paul's letter to Titus.

You are entitled to disagree with most of the rest of this book because so much of it is a matter of counsel based on experience, but in this chapter let us all put ourselves under the scrutiny of the Holy Spirit. This is God's word and, therefore, calls only for our submission. The test paper is this:

> 'Teach the older men to be temperate, worthy of respect, self-controlled, and sound in faith, in love and in endurance. Likewise, teach the older women to be reverent in the way they live, not to be slanderers or addicted to much wine, but to teach what is good. Then they can train the younger women to love their husbands and children, to be self-controlled and pure, to be busy at home, to be kind, and to be subject to their husbands, so that no-one will malign the word of God' (Titus 2:2-5).

Join me in a little Bible study in this passage that the Lord has given especially for us, and let us ask the Lord to help us to apply what we learn to ourselves.

The test for older men

1. Temperance
We are to be sober and not drunkards. As age advances and its limitations become more frustrating, some men try to drown their feelings with excessive drinking. This is dishonouring to the Lord and in any case, since it does not remove the problem, it is a waste of time and money. Let us prove that the Lord Jesus Christ can enable us to overcome our discomforts and to be different from those who have no other solution but the temporary relief drinking might give.

2. Worthy of respect
This means that we are to be dignified, which drunkenness certainly is not. Some older men are tempted to 'let themselves go', to neglect their appearance, personal hygiene and behaviour so that other people begin to despise them. Just as we want children to act like children and not to be old before their time, in the same way, older men will earn respect by showing the wisdom, humility and dignity that befits their age.

3. Self-controlled
This is conduct controlled by wisdom, especially wisdom gleaned both from the Bible and from experience. In particular, Christian men must be above suspicion in their relationships with children and young women. Self-control also includes the wise use of our tongues and the taming of our tempers.

4. Sound, healthy
As the days go by it is very easy to become careless about our physical health through lack of exercise or attention to our diet. The same applies to our spiritual well-being. Spiritual health can only be maintained by prayer and diligent application of the Scriptures, so we must not neglect our daily meeting with the Lord.

5. Sound in faith

Healthy faith has a clear grasp of the doctrines of Scripture and through them a strong and firm confidence in God who is revealed in those doctrines. Younger people look to us for an example of genuine trust in God in every aspect of life.

6. Sound in love

This is love for God the Father and for our Lord and Saviour, Jesus Christ; love for the gospel; love for God's people and for those who are lost because they are outside of Jesus Christ. This love should have grown through the years, but it needs constant renewing, which is one good reason for continuing attendance at the Lord's Supper for as long as we can.

7. Sound in endurance

We may not tread so firmly as we used to and may even begin to stumble and fall, but our experience of God's faithfulness and of the hazards of church life as well as its blessings, should enable us to be patient and unwavering in our spiritual life.

The test for older women

1. Reverent in the way they live

This simply means that they are to be serious in trying to please God in every way, their general bearing, their relationships, their dress and their whole programme of life.

2. Not to be slanderers

If they are living on their own, it is terribly easy to fill the time with unworthy thoughts about other people and to convert these thoughts into gossip at an early opportunity. Ladies are usually better than men in homely conversation with neighbours; this can be used wrongly, but it can also be a wonderful opportunity for the gospel.

3. Not addicted to much wine

The sight of a 'tipsy' man or woman is sickening and to be abhorred. Christians are to find their consolation, encouragement and cheer in the Lord and not in liquor. We are to be Spirit-controlled and not spirit- controlled!

4. Teach what is good

Perhaps the early church gave older women responsibility in teaching newly marrieds the way to seek a healthy and harmonious, God-honouring family life (see 1 Timothy 5:4), and it may be that our modern church life fails to use them as we should. Perhaps if we did, young pastors would be less exposed to the temptations and hazards involved in private counselling sessions with young women. Apart from that there are many one-to-one opportunities for informal advice and our older ladies should not shrink from giving help where it is needed or asked for. Some younger wives may spurn such help, but those who seriously want to please the Lord in their young family life, will value the guidance that comes from a knowledge of Scripture and from long experience.

Well, that is the test. How well have you done? School teachers have always been on safe ground when they put on their reports 'could do better'! If we are honest as we test ourselves by the standard of Scripture, we will admit that we 'could do better', and submit ourselves afresh to the Lord for his enabling.

CHAPTER ELEVEN

Too Close For Comfort?

Take another look at that gnarled old tree in the centre of an eastern courtyard. The children play around it and climb on its branches, while the grateful housewife gleans its fruit each year without fail (Psalm 92:14). Not beautiful, mis-shaped in places and reaching the end of its usefulness, but still much loved, and the day of its being cut down anticipated with sorrow and regret. It is at the heart of the family and part of its everyday life.

That is the picture of elderly people within the life of a family, not highly disposable nuisances, or problems you hope will go away if you ignore them, but at the heart of the family and amazingly essential to the completeness of family life.

Opinions differ about what is called the 'extended family'; some people believe that we should adopt an ancient tradition of older people remaining in the same household. Undoubtedly, in many cases, this would solve the problems of caring for elderly relatives when they become frail or infirm. Also this arrangement recognises the value and possible usefulness of older members within the family circle.

But there are a number of obstacles to this working out in practice. For example, if all the other members of the family are away from home during the daytime at school, college or work, the caring element is less realistic. Also, when the family is at home, they may all be too busy to give time to the needs of the older person. In these days, people are often quickly out again in the evenings at church functions, visiting friends or at social activities. If the older person is reasonably active, being alone during the day will not be a great problem, but if he or she is house-bound, loneliness can cause distress. All this depends very much on circumstances and the personalities of all those involved.

The older we get the less we appreciate the noise of boisterous youngsters, and possible irritations abound; differing musical tastes or preferences of TV programmes being high on the list. Likewise, attitudes to money: if you were brought up to darn socks or mend stockings you will have to get used to this throwaway culture. Your grand-children will never have seen a darning mush-room, much less will they know what it was for. All these differ-ences will be more acute if your family members are not believers.

This may be the biggest test of our Christian character we have ever had to face, and we will need all the grace the Lord gives us to cope with it happily and with contentment. You may want to quote the fifth commandment that requires children to

> 'honour your father and your mother ... ' (Exodus 20:12).

This obligation still stands and children are answerable to God for the way they treat their parents, but it is obvious that in later years, the way children obey this command, is different from when they were youngsters. Nevertheless, even in those earlier years, parents need to merit the honour of their children, as Paul wrote,

> 'Fathers do not embitter your children, or they will be-come discouraged' (Colossians 3:21).

Our need to be worthy of our children's respect becomes, if any-thing, even more important in later years; if we want to receive honour, we must ourselves be honourable!

Let us think about some of the things we may do that make it difficult for our loved-ones to respect us, no matter if we live with them or at a distance from them. For instance, we can become unreasonably demanding or even downright selfish. We should remember that they have their lives to live, and that they have pressures to cope with that we probably can't begin to understand. When we bear that in mind, we will ask ourselves if we really do need what we are persistently demanding.

Now I know that, unfortunately, some younger relatives seem to do as little as they can to help us and if they do anything, it is done with bad grace. In that case we must try to find ways of encouraging them to help us, or it may be right to share the problem with a pastor or mature Christian friend. What is certain is that we are unlikely to improve the situation by complaining or by loudly demanding our rights. We will return to that subject in chapter 21.

Then, we must also be careful about interfering in family disputes, no matter whether adults or children are involved: they have to work the problems out for themselves. This means that you and I should keep quiet even when we are tempted very strongly to intervene.

We may disapprove of the way our grand-children are being trained or, we may think, of their lack of training, and again we are tempted to intrude. As David Gay suggests, it is right for us to give counsel and advice if we are consulted, but apart from that it is all too easy to make things worse by being constantly critical, or even trying to take matters into our own hands. This requires a great deal of patience, and we must exercise self control as the Lord enables us.

It is very important to be positive in our attitudes and to be constructive and encouraging as often as we can. Best of all we should try to be cheerful, rather than grumpy or morose, and to be thankful, rather than taking the help we receive for granted. We cannot express our gratitude too often, and we need to be looking out for every opportunity to encourage the younger family members in what they are striving and hoping for.

If you are living with one of your children along with grand-children, you don't need me to tell you that this is by no means easy. But do try to see your situation as a great opportunity to prove to yourself and to them, the Lord's enabling grace. That gnarled old tree, if you will pardon the comparison (!) must go on bearing fruit, spiritual fruit — to the end.

CHAPTER TWELVE

The Honourable Parent

Maybe you are not living under the same roof as your children because you have been able to make a decision not to do so, like one eighty year old widower who writes:- 'having witnessed outside of my immediate family, the cloying effect of aged relatives on their children and grandchildren, I am determined to be independent of my loving family, in so far as daily living is concerned.' So we may decide that there is good reason for us to live separately from our children, if our health is good enough and our finances can cope with it. Sometimes, the burden of caring for elderly parents rests on children who are themselves past retirement age and who may be in need of help; even if they want to care for us and even like us to share their home, their own situation prevents them from doing so.

We should not be dogmatic about whether ageing parents should live with their children, but, as we have already seen, there are principles that apply to all of us, no matter whether we live under the same roof, in the same road, or at a greater distance. As I suggested in chapter 11, our task is to be 'honourable' parents, by which I mean we are to apply Christian standards to our relationship with our family, in such a way as to earn their respect, their love and their help in time of need.

The 80 year old man I quoted earlier doesn't allow being separated from his family to diminish his interest in them. 'I have two married sons and two daughters-in-law and seven grandchildren. It has been my habit for several years to phone each one on their birthday ... accuracy of age being especially important to children for present-buying ... '

Perhaps the most difficult situation to cope with is trying to relate to younger family members who are not Christians. We will want to keep in close touch with them so that they do not lose the benefit of our Christian witness. No matter how much we try to do this, there will be the constant danger of drifting apart because our interests are so different.

Practical problems arise such as our unconverted relatives wanting to visit us at times when they know full well we would prefer to be in a church meeting. This may be sheer carelessness on their part or it could be the only time they are able to come. We need to ask ourselves whether it is more honouring to the Lord to insist on going to our service, or to deprive ourselves of that privilege for the sake of keeping up good relationships with our loved ones. If we choose to miss a service, we should leave our visitors in no doubt that we only do so with the greatest reluctance.

If members of our family are not converted, they will not thank us for 'ramming religion down their throats', but they should be made aware that we pray for them, are ready to answer their questions about our faith, and we should commend our Lord to them by our loving attitudes. We remember that Timothy heard about the teaching of the Bible, not only from his mother, but also from his grand-mother (2 Timothy 1:5; 3:14-15), and it may be we will have the opportunity to tell our grandchildren about the Lord if and when their parents neglect this privilege. We can give them presents of books about the Bible, or about famous Christian people.

We are meant to enjoy our grandchildren, nieces and nephews, and the Bible says that they are a sign of God's blessing to us —

> 'May the LORD bless you from Zion all the days of your life; may you see the prosperity of Jerusalem, and may you live to see your children's children' (Psalm 128:5-6).

The generation gap seems to get wider and wider, making our contact with the young people in the family difficult to sustain, but as a general rule, it is still true that if we set out to enjoy them, they will respond and enjoy our company too.

Just occasionally I have had a phone call from one of my two daughters that has begun 'Dad, we think you should ... '. Immediately my alarm bells have started ringing! Those two girls have been discussing my welfare and they have agreed what they would say to me. Most probably they have also talked it over with their husbands, so I have four of them ganging up on me! When this kind of thing happens, we must pocket our pride and be willing to take advice. The first time it happens it is rather a shock, and you realise that your relationship with your children is taking on a different and interesting new shape. Of course, you have not lost your ability to think for yourself, but don't close your mind to the possibility that you may be wrong. If perchance, after careful thought, you can't accept the advice, be sure to be generous in your reply, thanking them for their love and concern, and telling them not to hesitate to be always open with you.

When King Solomon wanted to impress his son with the blessings that go with godly living, he told him that he had learned them from his own father —

> 'When I was a boy in my father's house, still tender, and an only child of my mother, he taught me and said "lay hold of my words with all your heart; keep my commands and you will live"' (Proverbs 4: 3-4).

Now suppose his son could have replied 'and look at your father; what good has all this religion done him? He is cross and grumpy all the time and he is always criticising me; he never has a good word for me to encourage me. I don't like him.' If that had happened, all attempts to persuade the boy that a godly life leads to true happiness would be a waste of time. In fact, Solomon's experience led him to say

> 'Children's children are a crown to the aged, and parents are the pride of their children' (Proverbs 17:6).

So it is possible for us to live in such a way that our children love us and are proud of us — there's the challenge! We really must believe, that grandads and grandmas are an important part of family life and a significant influence in the conversion of the younger generation.

CHAPTER THIRTEEN

Dusted Off!

'Who is Mrs Knowles?' Everyone was talking about Mrs Knowles who was due to pay her annual visit to the church. I didn't know this lady, but I could almost detect a feeling of reverence for her in those who did, when the word went round 'Mrs Knowles is coming!' So I wanted to know who she was and why there was so much excitement about her coming visit. I knew she was a member of the church but she was now living in another part of the country. I discovered that she was very aged and that she was living with other members of her family, but her life was lonely because the family were not believers and were totally unsympathetic to her spiritual inclinations. So much I learned, but my problem remained; why was she so lovingly admired? Then, the Sunday came when this lady was gently led into the morning service and immediately my problem was solved. Even from the platform I could sense her extra-ordinary blend of humility, joy, thankfulness and godliness. She was like a magnet; people were drawn to her and her presence alone had a tremendous impact on us all.

One sign of a healthy church is that it has a good range of all ages, from babies, to those in the later stages of life, and where all are in harmony. In one church where I pastored, a visiting preacher roundly told the older people they should step aside and give way to the younger people. In the after-church coffee session, I was fascinated to see perhaps the most modern of the younger generation, talking to the preacher, and to overhear her say to him, 'we have a good working relationship between the young and the old in this church already.' I was proud of her!

I know that often the young people can be headstrong and aggravating, and can try to ride rough-shod over those with longer experience. That is a problem for church leaders, but the question here is about the place in church life of those who are ageing and whose powers are diminishing. The answer has to be that there is a positive place for such, and that a church is impoverished if it has no people of the older generation in its membership.

There is no doubt that the most important thing is what we are. How wonderful it would have been if Mrs. Knowles had been able to attend her church every Sunday! What a great influence for good!

Miss Smith was an elderly single lady living on her own in a council bungalow. There was nothing about her that would draw attention, and she was not specially gifted, but everyone knew her; she was Aunt Carrie to all, and her home was the constant focal point for young people at which to meet. Her influence on them was wise and godly, but why was this? Why did people so often say, 'I must go to see Aunt Carrie?' The answer has to be simply that it was because of what she was, a sincere godly woman, with no hint of guile, but an Irish sense of humour.

Many people would agree with Shakespeare —

> 'Crabbed age and youth cannot live together
> Youth is full of pleasure, and age is full of woe.'
>
> *(The Passionate Pilgrim)*

— but in church-life with God's help, we can prove such notions to be wrong. Older people in a church, just by reason of being there, are living examples of what Jesus Christ can do and of his keeping power. By their lives they confirm the message being preached, especially if they have been Christians for 40, 50 or more years.

What a pity then, when we spoil that idea by earning a reputation for criticising those who are younger, or who are in positions of leadership. How often older people have been seen as negative, always opposing anything new. You may say, 'surely there are times when we need to speak out to stop them doing something foolish?'

The answer is that there may be such times, but we need to bear three things in mind. The first is this; if we are always against everything and always difficult to please, then when the really important issues arise, younger people will not be well disposed to us, and less willing to listen. We need to develop a more positive approach by being generally cheerful and hopeful, and by using every opportunity to encourage those who are doing the work and bearing the burdens. Let us assure them of our prayers, and look out for opportunities to tell them how well they're doing, and how much we appreciate their efforts. Then, at least we may hope they will listen when we raise serious questions about what they are doing or plan to do.

The second important thing is for us to be mature enough to distinguish matters of biblical principle from our own cherished preferences or traditions. If we can point to Scripture, we are on firm ground and the church should heed our warning. But if the issue is about tradition or our likes and dislikes, then we are still entitled to express our point of view, but most probably we will find that the church is now facing problems or opportunities we never encountered and the world around us is changing more rapidly than ever. We must allow the people who are actually doing the work, to know how best to do it. That is not easy, but we must try!

The third thing is being as useful as we can and yet knowing when to give up. Again, that is not easy! How often a musician, or the leader of some part of church life, has hung on to the job out of sheer pride when they were 'past it', with the rather dubious claim 'the Lord hasn't told me to give up'. This is even more serious when a suitable younger person is patiently waiting in the wings. A church once gained the services of a young organist because he was not allowed even to practise on the organ of the church he had been attending — its elderly player was in total possession of the instrument. The decision is often difficult to reach and there are no rules, except that we be sensitive to giving up too soon, or hanging on too long. I went to a church recently where the piano was played superbly by a lady in her eighties and the organ by someone very much younger. Sometimes other members love us too much to tell us that we should retire and they will protest when we say that is what we are going to do. Do not be deceived, try to look at the whole situation and do what is best for the church no matter what your own feelings may be.

Having said all those things, we can often still be useful in the church in other ways. As we suggested in chapter 8, why not ask your elders if there is something you can do, within the limits of your physical state? They may be able to use you in counselling or visiting. There may be copying, paper-folding or tea making. We should try to make ourselves useful so long as we are able to do so.

As we have mentioned before, in Psalm 92: 12-14 the writer takes the picture of a domestic palm tree and applies it to older people in the church. Just as the tree was still profitable to a family after many years of fruit bearing, so older people can be at the heart of church life, bearing the fruit of godliness and usefulness —

> ' ... planted in the house of the Lord, they will flourish in the courts of our God. They will still bear fruit in old age, they will stay fresh and green.'

After I retired, the church of which I was a member launched a new work, and I was asked to help with the preaching. The person who dealt with the notices on the first morning remarked that they had 'dusted him off' for the purpose! In the same church the young people's work came to a time of transition, and temporary mature leadership was required. They called on a retired couple, who were very surprised, since they had no previous experience of youth work. The young people loved them and the move was just what was needed.

Perhaps the demands of work and family in the past have prevented you from playing a part in church life. Now you are retired, this may well be your opportunity. Some people who have spent all their adult lives having to work for payment, find it difficult to make the transition to voluntary work. We need to tell ourselves that now is the time to serve the Lord freely and selflessly.

There is quite a difference between working in a paid situation and serving voluntarily with other volunteers. The basis of paid work is a contract that sets out times, standards and agreed terms. Working in a voluntary setting means not grumbling about those who are not so keen, or whose standard of work leaves a little to be desired. In church life, we do our best to please the Lord and others should do the same, but we have to learn the lesson the Lord gave to Peter who pointed to another disciple and asked 'what will this man do?' Jesus replied

> 'what is that to you, you must follow me' (see John 21:21-22).

That is typical of serving the Lord in the work of the church, no matter whether we are young or old.

CHAPTER FOURTEEN

Prayer

Her name was Mrs. Skinner; she was a widow and her health was doubtful enough to keep her housebound most of the time. In any case, she lived in a village four or five miles from the chapel where she was a member, she had no means of transport, and furthermore, she had little or no fellowship from day to day, since there were no other believers near at hand. Before I visited her, as I did about once a month, I had to be precise in my preparation because I knew that after the usual courtesies, I would be subjected to the most detailed examination about everything and everyone in the life of the church. She had her list of people and events that she had been praying about, and she wanted to know how the Lord had been answering her prayers.

What an encouragement that was to a young, inexperienced pastor. Those visits were a pleasure and a tonic. Mrs. Skinner knew that, though she was not able to attend services, much less able to be physically involved in the church activities, she was in the front line of the spiritual battle, and I knew that the Lord was using her prayers toward the spiritual blessings he gave us.

You will notice that Mrs. Skinner did not wait to be informed about what was happening in the church, nor did she need to be reminded to pray for us. Too often older people say 'nobody tells me what's going on' or, 'I don't hear about the church these days'. We should remember that our elders and their colleagues are very busy and that we may not be the first people on their minds. Mrs. Skinner took the initiative; she did not want to know what was going on so that she could criticise; she demanded news so that her prayers could be informed.

Job, that great Old Testament character, regularly prayed for his children:

> 'When a period of feasting had run its course, Job would send and have them purified. Early in the morning he would sacrifice a burnt offering for each of them, thinking, "Perhaps my children have sinned and cursed God in their hearts." This was Job's regular custom' (Job 1:5).

This is a great ministry. If our children are believers, we should be concerned for their growth in the knowledge of God and his ways. You can be sure the devil is trying to stumble them one way or another. Perhaps they are in danger of succumbing to worldliness or materialism, or it may be their marriage is under stress and you are not aware of it. Perhaps their children are causing them anxiety, or they have money problems, or their Christian work is discouraging. Because they are Christians, they do not need our prayers any the less.

When our children are not believers, we may have been praying for them for many years and there is no apparent change. The temptation is to give up in despair, but this we must never do. Roger Palms records that, 'To the parents of a 15 year old I've said, "don't ever give up on your children". To a parent of a 30 year old I've said, "don't ever give up on your children". And to a parent of a 45 year old, "don't ever give up on your children."'

As we become more and more immobile, we may think we will have more time for prayer. But the reality is that everything else takes much longer to do than it used to. Dressing in the morning, cleaning the rooms, preparing meals — they all leave us short of breath and often in need of an afternoon nap! Before we know where we are, the day has gone. All this is natural and we must not be cross with ourselves about it or lose patience; better to have a good laugh about what old fogies we have become! But what about opportunities for prayer? If our lives as Christians have always been bounded by morning and evening prayer, it will not be difficult to continue that practice, or we may be able to lengthen the sessions. Whatever may be our situation, if we think seriously about prayer it will be almost certainly possible to spend more time than we did in the past.

Concentration in prayer is a problem at all ages, and it does not go away with age; the mind still wanders but in different directions from when we were younger. Many years ago I developed the habit of saying my prayers, either in a whisper, or aloud. This is a tremendous help and I commend it to you if you are able to have your private prayer time away from other people's ears. At first, you may not care for the sound of your own voice, especially if it is beginning to croak! But it is well worth persevering.

Another aid to concentration might be having a number of shorter prayer times instead of one or two longer ones. This will be especially helpful if pain disturbs us. In chapter 7 we said that it is good to have a kind of structure in mind for each day, and that structure should include set times when we seek the Lord. We should be flexible about times. Just recently, Georgie and I decided we were too tired at bedtime for that to be best for our evening prayer. So now we come to the Lord together at tea time. Another element in our structure could be having different purposes in prayer at certain times of the day. For example, we might set aside one session for worship, praise and thanksgiving, then another session for praying over missionary news, and then another for intercession for our own church and family. Each of us, whether with family or partners, or on our own, can work this out for ourselves.

When we were younger, perhaps when we were baptised we sang, 'O Jesus I have promised to serve thee to the end.' Now we are discovering the importance of the words 'to the end'. The challenge of keeping that promise has taken on a different form, but it is no less demanding; we might even think that it is more difficult. It is possible that we have, unthinkingly, assumed that our needs will not be so great as we advance in years, that experience will save us from drifting or even falling. But, the fact is, we have not experienced growing old before; there is an entirely new set of hopes, fears, temptations, joys and sorrows. So it is that we need constantly to draw grace and enabling from the Lord, to lay hold of his promises and make them our own.

Not only do we need to pray for our own spiritual needs, but it is good to have a positive view of why we are where we are. Wherever it is, God intends us to be witnesses and to be ready for him to use us in the conversion of neighbours, friends, fellow patients, or residents in establishments for the elderly. This too, needs to be included in our prayer concerns, that the Lord will guide us and use us, teaching us what to say and when to say it.

If prayer is a weapon in the Christian warfare, then it follows that when we pray, we are in the front line of the spiritual conflict. So we must rid our minds of the attitude that says, 'all I can do is pray', as though this was second, third or even fourth best, far less important than what we call active Christian service. If only we could realise that this is the most important ministry of all, we would be much more diligent in prayer than, alas, most of us are. Let church elders and leaders, missionaries at home and overseas be assured of our constant faithful intercessions before God on their behalf.

CHAPTER FIFTEEN

Lonely?

Does this ring a bell? 'I go all around the shops and get a loaf, which is really all I need, and then go and have a cup of tea in the cafe upstairs. I don't see a soul I know and don't speak to anyone. By the time I've trailed all the way home again and gone up in the lift to my flat on the twelfth floor, I feel ready to jump out of the window' (CARE Action File).

But it doesn't have to be like that! Beryl lived with her sister Gladys, both were senior citizens, and she was asked if they felt lonely. 'No', she said, 'I can honestly say we don't feel lonely, we have the Lord as our friend and he has promised to be with us, and we found over the years that he never leaves us nor forsakes us, so we can't possibly feel lonely, and we keep occupied so that we haven't the time to be lonely.' But what if she lived on her own, would that make a difference? 'I don't think it would' she said, 'I should certainly miss having someone in the house — I did have an experience of being alone for quite a few weeks — I thought I would feel lonely, and I wasn't looking forward to it in the least, but I didn't feel lonely, and I was absolutely amazed at how the time went and the sense of the Lord's presence with me was just wonderful'.

Some years later Beryl's sister Gladys had died, what would she say now? Did she still feel the same way? Her answer was, 'at first, naturally I missed her and must confess I felt sorry for myself, but I began to realise what it meant for Gladys to be relieved of her suffering and to be with Christ which is far better.' Then, Beryl summed up her feelings with a verse of a Christian song:

By proving the Lord's compassion
I proved how he keepeth his word;
I'm proving each hour the marvellous power
Of Jesus, my Saviour and Lord.

You will notice how Beryl had the natural feelings of sadness and fear. It is not wrong to feel like that, much less is it sinful even to feel lonely. The Christian experience does not make us unnatural people, but the presence of Christ enables us, not merely to put up with loneliness but to overcome it.

Roger Palms gives us this helpful nugget — 'what about people who have always lived alone? Sometimes it is difficult for a single person to muster sympathy for a husband or wife who loses a spouse after forty-five or fifty years of marriage. "Now they're where I've always been." says the single person. Whether they've always been alone or are alone for the first time in decades, many have discovered that it is good to be alone. God's promise "... your Maker is your husband —" (Isaiah 54:5) takes on a special meaning for them ... "never will I leave you, never will I forsake you" (Hebrews 13:5) has a new dimension to it.'

Most often, when we face the problems of life, there are things we can do to help ourselves, for example, lonely people can seek out other lonely people. Two things, Christ's friendship for us, and our's for others, are nicely put together in the proverb —

> 'A man who has friends must himself be friendly but there is a friend who sticks closer than a brother' (Proverbs 18:24 NKJV).

Whether or not that is the best translation, what it says is very wise. One of the most important questions elderly people, living on their own, must ask themselves is how they can be friendly to others. Better than sitting alone pitying ourselves, is thinking of ways we can develop friendships. If we are physically fit, we can throw off our natural reserve and visit another lonely person, not just once, but regularly, if it is appreciated. One older person living on her own has written 'when left on one's own suddenly ...

it might be a good idea to look around and see if they could befriend someone else in similar circumstances or in need of a friend — not to keep themselves to themselves and feel sorry about their own circumstances. There are so many lonely people around.'

If you are confined to your home, or going out is difficult, then you could think how to invite someone to visit you, perhaps another older person or even someone younger. In this connection, Ivy in her nineties has an interesting piece of advice. 'Continue to care for your personal appearance, it is an effort, but to always look neat, tidy or even smart, keeps you on your toes.' Pastors visit all kinds of people in all kinds of condition and they have to be blind to personal appearance. But if we expect friends to look forward to visiting us and to enjoy our company, we can help ourselves by taking Ivy's advice.

As we grow older it is not always easy to keep our rooms clean and tidy. Our friends will understand this and they may offer to help. If they do, be sure to let them do so with good grace. I have paid regular pastoral visits to homes where I have been offered tea, knowing full well the cups would be so soiled as to make one feel sick. Such people can hardly complain if other visitors are rare.

Another hazard to avoid is possessiveness. Sometimes older people are so keen to have visitors that they embarrass their friends with too much pressure to stay longer. If our friends can come again next week, it is not wise for us to press for them to return tomorrow. If they can only manage monthly visits then we should be thankful for that — it is better to have friends call on us less often than we hope, than for them not to come at all. Unreasonable pressure tends to put people off, so let us assure people that we want them to come to see us, but let us also be content with the time they feel able to give us in their busy lives. If they stay for only five minutes, don't complain about this being too short. We have time on our hands, but we must remember that they are most probably very busy people.

It is also very important for us not to overburden our visitors with our problems. People living on their own tend to bottle up their worries and complaints and then to unload them on their first unfortunate visitor. Our friends naturally ask us about ourselves, and there is good reason for us to tell them the truth and to share our problems with them. But as soon as possible, we should try to turn the conversation away from ourselves and talk about the things that interest our visitors, such as their family, their work in the church, or their recent holidays. Let us try not to earn a reputation for being boring because we talk endlessly about ourselves.

There is always the possibility of forming a close friendship with another lonely person, someone with whom you spend time sharing at a more intimate level than is possible with an occasional visitor. Just being together can be a great blessing, and such a friendship can include prayer times, playing Scrabble, or watching videos. Experience shows that sometimes such close friendships can result in love and marriage between two people who never thought of such a possibility. This is wonderful when it happens, but an increasing number of older people are proving that there is great comfort and benefit in close, morally sound, friendships that stop short of wedding bells.

There are many other ways of overcoming loneliness. If we have grandchildren, or know of other children living nearby, how about keeping some toys or other interests at hand to draw them to us? There may be a limit to the length of time we can cope with them, but we can enjoy them in small doses!

Then there is the telephone. Regular calls to relations or friends bring them nearer to us, but we need to be careful of making our calls at inconvenient times, and of making them too often and too long.

We can also make judicious use of radio and television. The response of the public to the recent murder of a popular television presenter, shows how such people can become like friends to us. Some people are actually given to 'talking to' their radio or television, so close do the presenters seem to come to them! My housebound mother-in-law had come to believe that television was an instrument of the devil, and of course we know only too well that Satan is using it to spread heresy and corruption. But after much effort we managed to persuade her that the instrument in itself is not evil and can be useful. The result was that she enjoyed many regular wholesome programmes and became an authority on West Indian fast bowlers, of whom she did not approve!

CHAPTER SIXTEEN

Neglected?

People who live on their own often feel lonely and neglected; maybe you're one of them. Perhaps you are a widow or a widower, a single man or woman, and the older you get, the sense of isolation can eat into your mind until you begin to think that everyone has forgotten you and you feel thoroughly neglected.

'I haven't seen anyone for a week' — 'no-one has been to see me from the church. They've fogotten all about me.' Every pastor is familiar with the refrain, and sad to say, such complaints are sometimes justified. This should not happen. No church member should ever have good reason to feel lonely, and care for the elderly should surely be very high on the list of pastoral priorities. But it is not wise to believe all we hear. As we chat with someone who has made such complaints, if we wait long enough, questions begin to arise in our minds like, 'how did he know that, if no-one from the church has been to see him?' — 'she must have seen someone from the church within the last one or two days.' Naturally, we allow for memory failure, and we are too polite to point out that the church has not been so remiss as they were suggesting. As I said, every pastor knows the problem and learns how to deal with it.

One of the great blessings of belonging to a church is that we are very likely to have people visit us. Some churches are better at this than others; in some cases, the visiting of the lonely is left to individuals, who take the responsibility on themselves. In other churches, some kind of visiting rota is organised. We should be grateful for what is done, no matter whether it is planned or not.

All church members living on their own, value a visit from 'the pastor', but we should remember that pastors have increasingly, time-consuming burdens and we should not complain if their visits are few and far between, especially if we are well served by other elders, deacons or church members. If you feel you need a pastoral call, don't complain to others that the pastor hasn't come, rather send him a message that you would very much like to see him, if he can spare the time. Always remember that the gift of telepathy is not included in the gifts required of pastors, so if you don't tell him, how will he know you would like a visit?

So much depends on how fit and mobile we are, but in any case, the older we get the longer it takes to do things, and everything is much more trouble. This is true when it comes to going to meetings, outings or other events, and there is the temptation to refuse invitations because of the hassle of getting ready. Especially in winter time, or during bad weather, more clothes are needed and we begin to feel the whole thing is too much trouble. Churches try to organise lifts for us, and community organisations do what they can to make life interesting for people like us, to keep our minds active, and put us in touch with other people in the same situation as ourselves. If we refuse them, we must not complain of being neglected, but it is far better if we possibly can, to accept these invitations, and when we return home, we will often say to ourselves that it was worth the effort.

Having said that, we have to agree that there is a special problem about going out at night. Quite apart from the danger of stumbling in the dark, there is also an understandable fear of violence in these days. Such problems are normally overcome if we have the help of an able-bodied friend, but there is still the dislike of returning to an empty house, that in the winter time is cold, dark and always seems very depressing. It may be possible for whoever has been helping us, to add a little while to their commitment by coming into the house, and staying with us for a few moments. But they are all busy people, and to be fair, this may be too much to ask, so there may be no other way but to stay at home on cold, dark nights.

However much we try to avoid it, we are very likely to spend time alone, sooner or later. But being alone is not the same thing as being lonely, and with the Lord's help, we can overcome a sense of loneliness, so that we do not have miserable feelings of being neglected.

Many of us have an important lesson to learn. We may have been very active in business, family life, leisure pursuits, or church work and ministry; so busy in fact, that we have relied on them for our satisfaction. We may have relied on the Lord's work instead of on the Lord himself — a common mistake. Now, if we are wondering why we must spend time on our own, one answer certainly is, that the Lord wants us to enjoy fellowship with him in a deeper way than we have known before. In this way, as I have said, we may be alone, but not lonely.

CHAPTER SEVENTEEN

Fellowship

> 'How lovely is your dwelling place, O LORD Almighty! My soul yearns, even faints, for the courts of the Lord; my heart and my flesh cry out for the living God' (Psalm 84:1-2).

Perhaps those are the words of someone like you, deprived of Christian fellowship and worship with the Lord's people. In the last two chapters we have discussed how to overcome loneliness in a number of ways, including developing friendships. This is helpful in itself, but for a believer, it can remain at a very general and even superficial level, not embracing anything specifically Christian. Friendship may lead to fellowship, and it is a great pity if it does not do so. I know the word 'fellowship' is sometimes used about secular clubs, and what happens in public houses, but this is just another example of a Christian word being highjacked by non-Christian writers. Fellowship is the spiritual dimension of friendship, and this is what I want to explore with you now.

When older people are less able to attend the meetings of their church, they are tempted to neglect fellowship. I have three things in mind; personal prayer fellowship with the Lord, prayer with other believers, and also sharing the Scriptures with others. When a married couple are aged and no longer active in the life of the church, it is very important for them to work out spiritual fellowship together. Alas! One of the strangest things in modern Christian homes is the failure of husbands and wives to talk together about spiritual things. Equally strange is the fact, that when they do discuss such matters, it is so often at the initiative of the wife.

It is better that wives should take the lead than that nothing is done at all, but it is shame on the men! The Scriptures place the responsibility in your court:

> 'For the husband is the head of the wife as Christ is the head of the church, his body, of which he is the Saviour' (Ephesians 5:23),

so if you have neglected this privilege, now is the time to do something about it. One good way of doing this is to discuss your daily Bible reading and any notes you may use. Georgie and I pray separately in the mornings and together in the evenings. In the mornings we both use the same Bible notes, so at breakfast time, it is not unusual for the conversation to begin, 'what did you think of the notes this morning ... ?' There are many blessings in marriage, but surely the best of all, is the joy of talking together about the Lord and his truth. Many single people would sell all that they had for the blessing of a partner, with whom they could share their spiritual experience, while all too many, who have this opportunity, do not use it!

Even in the matter of our personal prayer life and fellowship with the Lord, it is useful to be able to share this with someone else. What I mean is this — when we're alone we can become slack in the regularity of our set times of prayer, but if we have agreed times for prayer with a spouse, or a relative in the home, it is not so easy to drift. But those living on their own, need to work out regular prayer times and make it a matter of conscience to stay with them.

One area of church life that we should miss very much, when we are less able to attend, is the Lord's Supper. If we do not feel the loss, there is surely something lacking in our spiritual state. Faced with this problem, some dear people have asked their 'pastor' to come to them, and 'give them the communion', and a few have agreed to do this, while most have declined. The reason why 'private communion' is not practised generally in evangelical churches, is that the Lord's Supper is intended to be, not only a time of communion with God, but also of fellowship with brothers and sisters in Christ, and that we cannot properly separate the two. An essential element in the Lord's Supper is its uniting, cleansing and sanctifying effect on the local church. However, there are churches where a group of members meet with those who are housebound to share a communion service, and if you're concerned about this, why not speak to your church leaders about it?

This leads on naturally, to the possibility of inviting your church to hold regular prayer meetings in your home. If your church normally has house groups, why not suggest that your house is a good venue? Just because it is your home, you do not have to take any kind of lead, and if you cannot afford tea and biscuits, don't worry about that. If they want refreshments, tell them that you are quite happy for the group to provide them.

A less official and similar idea is what has become known as 'prayer triplets'. In these, three people commit themselves to regular prayer, very often for specific needs. Perhaps the burden will be for the young people in the church, or for unconverted spouses of church members, or for the church leaders, or some demanding project the church is undertaking. The number 'three' is not absolute, and this is a way of uniting in fellowship with other people who are feeling lonely or neglected. Such an arrangement can take on a missionary responsibility, involving keeping in direct touch with missionaries, or missionary families, and asking the Lord to meet their needs.

Fellowship can also be enjoyed with others, even without their physical presence. One Christian senior citizen, with many years of being on her own writes, 'I am still in touch with a great number of friends, here and overseas — and being friends still as we grow older, this helps them and me to feel wanted and of use. I was told once, "a person who is wrapped up in himself makes a very small parcel," and I think that is true.'

If you are not able to attend meetings at your church, there are still many ways of feeling part of the fellowship. One of these ways is listening to recordings of the services. Many churches, even those that are quite small, do such recordings, and the fact that someone has to remember to keep you supplied, keeps you in their minds as well as providing you with the ministry. If you do not have a cassette player, take courage to tell your church why you need one; in these days it will be very surprising if nobody has one to spare.

One way or another let us be sure to maintain fellowship with the Lord and his people. Remember

> 'Then those who feared the LORD talked with each other, and the LORD listened and heard. A scroll of remembrance was written in his presence concerning those who feared the LORD and honoured his name. "They will be mine," says the LORD Almighty, "in the day when I make up my treasured possession … "' (Malachi 3:16-17).

CHAPTER 18

Older And Wiser?

'What are hoary hairs?' The question was asked recently in a young people's group. No doubt, they had been in a service, and come upon the line of a hymn, 'And when hoary hairs shall their temple adorn,' or, maybe it was the line from another hymn, — 'His work my hoary age shall bless when youthful vigour is no more.' To me, the surprising thing was, that no one in the group knew what these expressions meant, until I pointed to my own grey hairs to enlighten them! Perhaps, when these tell-tale signs of advancing years first come, we do not notice them, or we do not want to see them! The immediate re-action of some people is to refuse to admit what others see, or to find comfort in hair dye, or a wig. But, no matter what we do, we cannot put the clock back, so it is better to live with hoary hairs and to learn from them!

In Scripture, white hairs are used as a symbol of wisdom. For example, in the book of Daniel, there is a vision of the Ancient of Days —

> 'His clothing was as white as snow; the hair of his head was white like wool' (Daniel 7:9),

and in the book of Revelation, John saw the glory of Christ

> 'dressed in a robe reaching down to his feet and with a golden sash around his chest. His head and hair were white like wool, as white as snow ... ' (Revelation 1:13-14).

The apostle Paul gloried in God's wisdom,

> 'Oh, the depth of the riches of the wisdom and knowledge of God … ' (Romans 11:33),

and it is this that is portrayed in the symbol of white hair. This teaches us that age should mean wisdom — it should be true of us, that we are older and wiser! This was certainly the view of Elihu,

> 'I thought, "Age should speak; advanced years should teach wisdom"' (Job 32:7).

The reason for this is, obviously, that older people have had years of experience, from which they should have learned many lessons, especially about mistakes to avoid. Experience is valuable and should not be ignored by families, churches or society generally. This very morning, as I am writing, the Daily Telegraph reports, 'An insurance and pension company has told its executives aged over 50, that they can leave with enhanced early retirement packages, irrespective of their experience …' That seems to be a very foolish thing to do; it cannot be sane to leave each generation to make the same mistakes as earlier ones, which must happen where experience is despised.

'To whom can young women turn when problems seem overwhelming, whether a career decision, or abuse, or question of love? Who can give perspective? Not us, if we refuse to be time-balanced persons whom God wants to provide to those who are younger. A wise, and beautiful sixty-year old, or eighty-year old is attractive, and has much to offer to others' (Roger Palms — '*Celebrate life after 50*' — page 12-13).

A Salvation Army worker writes, 'We must never underestimate the value of older people in the house, community or the world. Older people have an accumulation of experience and wisdom which cannot be found in youth. They must not be ignored.'

This also is the value of a personal testimony such as the one given by David the Psalmist:

> 'I was young and now I am old, yet I have never seen the righteous forsaken or their children begging bread' (Psalm 37:25).

But, unfortunately, older people are not always wiser, and it is well to remind ourselves that it is not hoary hairs that give wisdom, but the Spirit of God, as Elihu went on to say:

> 'But it is the spirit in a man, the breath of the Almighty, that gives him understanding. It is not only the old who are wise, not only the aged who understand what is right' (Job 32:8-9).

This is a warning against presuming that we know best, just because of our age. We are never too old to learn, nor should we think that we are beyond the need to be corrected. Paul did not tell Timothy that he had no need to correct older members of the church, but he advised him how this should be done:

> 'Do not rebuke an older man harshly, but exhort him as if he were your father' (1 Timothy 5:1).

So, let us consider some of the things older people themselves need to learn. For example, we need to learn how to accept correction. How quickly we bridle when some one presumes to point out something in which we are wrong. How dare they criticise us, when we have so much experience behind us? None of us likes to be proved wrong no matter how old we are, but it is much more difficult to bear as we grow older. Let us constantly tell ourselves, that we do not have perfect wisdom, and that we never grow out of the obligation to show humility, and to learn from our mistakes.

Another lesson we must learn, is wisdom to know when to speak and when to remain silent. This is important if we are still able to attend church business meetings. We can so easily appear to be against everything new, so much so, that other members are no longer listening to what we say. But it is painful to remain silent, when our experience cries out against the folly of what is being proposed. Wisdom shows itself in our willingness to encourage where we can, and to choose the right subject, the right moment, and the right words to oppose something being planned.

This can also be a problem in family life, when we see children or grandchildren doing things which our experience tells us is unwise. How can we avoid unwelcome interference, and yet lovingly make our feelings known? It may be best to pray and be silent, or perhaps to pray for wisdom when and how to speak.

Undoubtedly, the best contribution older people can make to a discussion, is to help those involved to see aspects of the problem they may not be aware of, or have overlooked. Age tends to give the ability to see many sides of a question, learned from experience. Whether or not our opinion is asked, we may want to begin with, 'I think ... ', but very often it will be more effective and acceptable if we begin, 'have you thought about this. ...' ? There must be wisdom both in what we say and in the way we say it!

Then, there is wisdom needed to handle ourselves. Experience should have taught us how to cater for our mental and our physical needs. It is very foolish to drift along without thought about our way of life, and how our minds can be kept alert, and our bodies can be kept as fit for as long as possible. So, we must plan our reading with a view to a balanced mental diet of spiritual and profitable matter. We may have a liking for some kinds of books, such as, in my case, biographies, but let us be sure to explore the wonderful range of spiritual, biblical literature that is available to us. Likewise, our food intake and our physical exercise, need to be given consideration. There is no wisdom in neglecting our bodies.

CHAPTER NINETEEN

Doubt

One of the benefits of growing older is, that age throws new light on passages of Scripture. One example of this is the words of the apostle John, writing to his friend Gaius:

> 'Dear friend, I pray that you may enjoy good health and that all may go well with you, even as your soul is getting along well' (3 John 2).

At first sight, this seems to be the wrong way round; we would expect John to want Gaius's soul to be as healthy as his body. Certainly, in our early years, that would be the more appropriate desire, as so often our physical fitness outstrips our spiritual strength by a long way. So, why does John put Gaius's health first? There is no suggestion that Gaius was unwell at the time of receiving John's letter, so there must be some other explanation.

I suggest one possible reason is, that John, who was very aged at the time of writing, was learning from experience the effect that physical decline can have on our feelings about our spiritual state. David Gay deals with this, and he quite firmly says, 'the Christian must not confuse the physical and the spiritual.' The danger is this, when we are feeling physically unwell, we can, at the same time, feel sluggish about prayer and worship, and this in turn makes us question the reality of our spiritual state — we lose assurance. So, John wants Gaius to go on feeling well, so that his assurance will not be affected by physical decline as the days go by.

A younger person may be reading this with some surprise. They may be saying 'this should not happen — surely all the past experience of an older person should lead to an increasing assurance of God's love, and this should be sufficient to overcome the effects of age.' The answer to that is, 'yes, this certainly should be so, but they are forgetting one very important factor — Satan.' The evil one never gives up trying to undermine our faith, and the fight against him goes on to the very end. He seeks to turn any situation to his advantage, and this certainly includes our declining powers of concentration, or the distraction of persistent pain, or discomfort.

The answer to this situation is, first of all, to be aware of the possibility of it happening, and then we will be able to recognise the problem as it arises. Then we must tell the Lord how we feel, and ask him to help us to overcome it. We need to tell ourselves, very firmly, that it is possible for our bodies to decline while our soul is still strong and healthy. The place of peace is found in Jesus Christ — it always has been, and always will be. As we sing:

Not what I am O Lord, but what Thou art!
That, that alone can be my soul's true rest;
Thy love, not mine, bids fear and doubt depart,
And stills the tempest of my tossing breast.

(Horatius Bonar)

When your pastor calls and you tell him that you have lost your assurance, and have begun to doubt your salvation, don't be surprised if he immediately asks you about your appetite, whether you are sleeping well, and about your health generally. He knows that you can be mistaken in thinking that you have a spiritual problem, and he will soon tell you that your problem is not some sin or spiritual defect, but simply the effect of your ill health. He will assure you without any doubt, that God loves you.

Loneliness can have a similar bad effect upon our spiritual feelings. As David Gay points out, we can think we have been deserted by our friends, and this in turn leads us to think that God also has forsaken us. If we are on our own for long periods of time, we can very easily sit and brood and think all manner of foolish things, and once again the evil one will make sure that we do not snap out of it. We need to set our minds on the assurances the Lord has given us, that he will not leave us or stop loving us.

> '... God has said, "never will I leave you; never will I forsake you"' (Hebrews 13:5).

Another common cause of doubt in older people is the effect of recalling the sins of younger days. Our minds can easily slip into a groove in which past sins intrude upon us in horrible succession. David, the Psalmist, knew about this kind of thing as he prayed,

> 'remember not the sins of my youth and my rebellious ways' (Psalm 25:7).

In our moments of weakness, Satan will fix our thoughts on such things until they ensnare us with doubt about our salvation, and with fear of judgement. In the same Psalm, David tells how he escaped:

> 'my eyes are ever on the Lord, for only he will release my feet from the snare' (verse 15).

The antidote, no doubt, is always to keep our minds refreshed with the gospel. This is why it is so important for us to maintain Christian fellowship, as I suggested in chapter 17. The great truth of the gospel is, that the 'blood and righteousness' of Jesus Christ cover all our sins forever. Our past sins, our present sins, our future sins, all come within the scope of the assurance that

> ' ... the blood of Jesus, his Son, purifies us from all sin' (1 John 1:7).

The great covenant, that is ratified by the blood of Jesus, has within it this solemn undertaking on God's part,

> 'I will forgive their wickedness and will remember their sins no more' (Hebrews 8:12).

So, we must not allow Satan to tell us that he has resurrected what God has buried — Satan is a liar and always has been.

When Paul, the apostle, recalled his terrible persecution of Christians in earlier years, he was full of regret, but he did not allow his thoughts to stop with regret. He says,

> 'I was shown mercy' (1 Timothy 1:16);

that was his resting-place and it must be ours too.

Another thing to remember is, that

> '...when we were still powerless, Christ died for the ungodly' (Romans 5:6).

If you feel weak, and age is making you feeble, and this is robbing you of your assurance of salvation, then bear in mind that Jesus Christ died for people like you. He gave his life for those who were helpless and totally unworthy of his love. So, if that is how you feel, you are in the best possible position to be assured that God loves you, and that his love will not desert you.

Doubt, and lack of assurance, can be very distressing and make us long for peace of mind and heart. When this happens, always remember, that you would never be worried about your spiritual state if you were spiritually dead! Think about that! It is only those who have spiritual life that have spiritual feelings, so the fact that you feel concerned about whether you are saved, or whether God still loves you, is sure proof that you are a child of God.

The great thing is always to fix your eyes on Jesus, and you can best do this through meditating on passages of Scripture. They have been given to us for this very purpose, to give us comfort and assurance. Here are some of them:

> ' ... God demonstrates his own love for us in this: While we were still sinners, Christ died for us' (Romans 5:8).

> '... I am convinced that neither death nor life, neither angels nor demons, neither the present nor the future, nor

any powers, neither height nor depth, nor anything else in all creation, will be able to separate us from the love of God that is in Christ Jesus our Lord' (Romans 8:38-39).

'Since, then, you have been raised with Christ, set your hearts on things above, where Christ is seated at the right hand of God. Set your minds on things above, not on earthly things. For you died and your life is now hidden with Christ in God' (Colossians 3:1-3).

'Let us fix our eyes on Jesus, the author and perfecter of our faith ... ' (Hebrews 12:2).

CHAPTER TWENTY

Fear And Worry

'Do not be afraid.' Our Lord offered this encouragement on many occasions, during his ministry; that fact surely indicates, that he was very much aware that all of us are prone to fear and worry. This is true for people of every generation, but no one will dispute, that the older we grow, the greater is our tendency to anxiety and foreboding. We are not to think of Jesus' words, as though they are on the same level as our inane 'cheer-up' or 'all the best'. Such words may be well meaning but most often they are more depressing than helpful. When Jesus says, 'don't be afraid', his counsel is based on his wisdom and power, his love and sympathy.

The things that worry us are, most often, those about which we are unable to do anything, which suggests that, so long as we think that we can cope, we tend not to be too worried. This also implies that normally we trust ourselves, instead of relying on the Lord, so that when we can no longer cope, our lack of faith is exposed. So we need to take ourselves in hand, and to ask why we are not trusting the Lord, who has promised to be with us to the end.

Let us think about some of the things that tend to cause older people to be afraid. For example, we worry about money; we wonder if we will be able to meet electricity, gas, insurance and other bills. Many elderly people have a strong sense of independence, and hate the idea of relying on the help of others or the state. Then there is the business of leaving enough to pay for our funeral. People, who are anxious about such things, are told that the welfare state exists to ensure that they do not die of starvation, and that their needs will be met. But this is very little consolation when we read, and hear stories, of senior citizens suffering great poverty and distress. Those who criticise such worry and call it sinful, only make matters worse, and they probably have never been in a situation in which they cannot see how to 'make ends meet'. It is easy to say, 'just trust in the Lord', but they should ask themselves if that is what they would do in such circumstances without a twinge of fear or anxiety.

There were four young men at the back of the service, with their mouths firmly shut, as the rest of the congregation sang with vigour —

Though vine nor fig tree neither
Their wonted fruit should bear,
Though all the field should wither,
Nor flocks nor herds be there,
Yet God the same abiding,
His praise shall tune my voice;
For, while in Him confiding,
I cannot but rejoice.

(William Cowper)

'You wouldn't, would you?' they challenged, 'you wouldn't rejoice if you were starving?' It was a fair question, and they were right to demand that we should be humble and honest about such things. At least one of them was later converted, and learned to trust the Lord implicitly to the end.

We also tend to worry about our health; the older we get, the more likely we are to be alarmed at the slightest twinge of pain, or the most innocent cough. If we're living on our own, we're likely to be very concerned about the possibility of being taken ill, and no-one else knowing about it. Also, we can so easily imagine we have all kinds of serious problems, or we watch every day for the tell-tale signs of some deadly disease. Of course, it is right for us to take reasonable precautions, such as having regular flu injections, or asking the doctor to check on pains or lumps that develop, but remember, that if we worry over every sneeze, people are less likely to believe us when some really serious symptoms arise.

Going into hospital for an operation gives rise to many fears. I thought I wasn't worrying about a hernia operation; I had been through the same thing some years earlier, so I could take this one in my stride. So I thought, until the doctors began doubting if they could operate, because my blood pressure had gone right up, and was refusing to return to its normal level! It seems that worry can be sub-conscious; how we need to rest in the Lord! But how can we do that?

The best antidote to worry that I know, is to remind myself that when I became a Christian, the all-powerful, all-wise, all-loving God, made himself my heavenly Father, and took on the total responsibility for my life in all its needs, both spiritual and physical, for time and eternity. This was our Lord's wonderful teaching in the Sermon on the Mount,

> 'your heavenly Father knows...' (Read it all — Matthew 6:25-34).

When fear or worry begin to assail us, we need to relax in our Father's arms as children. When our situation seems to contradict his love and wisdom, and we begin to chafe or even rebel, we should recall that this is just how a screaming child feels in its mother's arms — 'everything is wrong, it hurts, I don't like it, if only she would listen to me!' By far and away, the best thing for that child is to give up screaming, and to be resigned to the mother's love and care. For us, by far and away the best thing is to

> 'be still before the LORD and wait patiently for him' (Psalm 37:7).

As we 'rest in the Lord', we can take note of two pieces of advice that have come to me from older friends. One of them writes: 'in my youth I was instructed that grace is not given to anticipate troubles ...' We are prone to cross our bridges before we get to them, which means that we worry today about what may happen tomorrow, and we are afraid that we may not be able to cope with problems that in the end do not occur, or if they do, are very much in the future. Our friend is right to say that we will not be given grace today, for what may or may not happen tomorrow.

Another friend, well advanced in years, comments on what ailing older people say, — 'oh well, what can you expect at our age?' She says, 'my reaction to that is, don't expect anything, take a day at a time' — and others have said the same thing to me. This really follows from our last paragraph, and it gives meaning to each day. If we are always worrying about what may happen tomorrow, next week, or next year, we are robbing ourselves of the enjoyment of what God has in store for us today.

Something that we have not mentioned, that weighs heavily on the minds of some elderly folk, is regret about wasted time in the past. This may be the godless years before they became Christians, which they now see were not spent in a profitable way, and so they assume that they were useless. It may be that we think, even since we became Christians, much of our time has been wasted. So one way or another, we brood over our regrets about the past, our sins, our wasted time, our disappointments about what might have been. This is a particularly futile occupation and is, in itself, a terrible waste of time, because there is absolutely nothing we can do about it. The way to put these regrets to rest, is to confess them to the Lord, and to know that they come within the total scope of his forgiveness, on the basis of the death of Jesus on our behalf. There is a helpful verse in the prophecy of Joel,

> 'I will repay you for the years the locusts have eaten ...' (2:25).

The locusts had destroyed the crops, and left the Israelite people without an adequate harvest, but now they were restored to God's favour, he promised to make up for lost time, presumably with bumper crops. We can apply this in the words of David Gay, 'an aged Christian can experience a glorious spiritual reviving in his closing years.' Furthermore, we can say that those years, though regrettable, were not entirely wasted, because during that time we learned lessons and had experiences that God has already woven into our spiritual development, and he will continue to do so.

CHAPTER TWENTY ONE

Rights And Lefts

> 'If anyone does not provide for his relatives, and especially for his immediate family, he has denied the faith and is worse than an unbeliever' (1 Timothy 5:8).

Thank God for all those organisations that exist to advance and defend the rights of senior citizens, and for all those families that thoughtfully and lovingly care for their older members. It is absolutely right for society to have the needs of older people high up on the welfare state agenda. It must be right for laws to be made to ensure justice for the most vulnerable among us, and for provision to be made for the elderly to be adequately housed and cared for. Families and churches have their responsibilities to look after their older members, and all this is clear from Scripture as James puts it

> 'religion that God our Father accepts as pure and faultless is this: to look after orphans and widows in their distress ... ' (1:27).

But this book is not primarily addressed to society, churches or families, but to those of us who are ageing and perhaps becoming dependent on others to help us or care for us. The question I want us to face here is, what is our attitude to our rights?

There can be no doubt that the prevailing atmosphere in the modern world is one of demanding rights and claiming compensation when people do not receive what they believe is their due. Let us ask ourselves if it is right for Christians to have such attitudes, or if this is one of those opportunities where we should be different and in so doing, bear a powerful witness. In his book *Christians in a Consumer Society,* John Benton has a chapter entitled 'the shocking impact of a contented Christian', and it seems to me that our attitudes to our rights has to be controlled by the requirement of Scripture, that we be contented people.

Perhaps the most challenging example given to us in the Bible is that of Paul, who when he was aged *and* confined to prison, wrote:

> ' ... I have learned to be content whatever the circumstances. I know what it is to be in need, and I know what it is to have plenty. I have learned the secret of being content in any and every situation ... ' (Philippians 4:11-12).

John Benton comments on the shock of 'finding an old, imprisoned and neglected apostle of a despised religion, and finding that he is totally at peace and aglow with a heavenly joy despite all his circumstances. No wonder the news of Christianity spread throughout the palace guard in Rome (Philippians 1:13). This man was like no other prisoner they had ever known!'

Please do not misunderstand what I am saying here. There is no reason at all why Christians should not fill in their claim forms for pensions, supplementary benefit, housing benefits or all the other helps there are in the welfare system. Nor is there any reason why we should not challenge the authorities if we think we are not being given what we're entitled to or are being treated unfairly. We should not become a burden on our family or church because we fail to claim what the government has provided for us. But at the same time, we must beware of reflecting the spirit of an age which is discontented, never satisfied, grasping, covetous and hostile to authority. Again, Paul spells out the Spirit-filled Christian's attitude

> '... godliness with contentment is great gain. For we brought nothing into the world, and we can take nothing out of it. But if we have food and clothing, we will be content with that' (1 Timothy 6:6-8).

The person who knows that heaven is but a short distance away, is not going to haggle endlessly about 'rights' in this passing world. This Christian attitude should extend to other areas of life. For example, Donald Howard writes, 'doctors, hospital staff or ministers are often targets for hostility. The minister has usually "neglected visiting". The doctor either made "a faulty diagnosis" or "performed an unnecessary operation". Of course, where there are firm grounds for such charges, the hostility is understandable, but it must nevertheless be brought to the Lord for removal. Like guilt, anger must be exposed, discussed and dealt with.' *(Christians Grieve Too).*

It is all too easy to sit and brood over what we think our family, our church or our doctor should have done or should be doing, and we may be right. But we should try to stop the build up of anger or resentment by remembering that there may well be good and satisfactory reasons for what has happened or what is not happening, and that in any case, all those involved, just like ourselves, are imperfect people. Furthermore, it is always very embarrassing when we have convinced ourselves that there has been carelessness or neglect, only to discover that our interests have been looked after all the time! We should constantly remind ourselves that other people do not exist simply and solely for our benefit; they have many other responsibilities and demands and they may even have as many worries and cares as we have, about which we know nothing.

Let us remember that doctors, welfare officials, church and family folk are not perfect. While we are brooding, it is a good idea to remember some of our own shortcomings and lapses in responsibility, and then we will be more ready to make allowances for those who try to help us and forgive their weaknesses and mistakes.

All this may seem very unbalanced or unfair, leaving mistakes uncorrected and more people to suffer as we have done because of failure to learn from what has happened. Let us suppose a case where a husband dies with a bone cancer which is not diagnosed as soon as it should have been, and then was not treated with the kind of attention it needed, and all this virtually admitted by doctors in the end. What should the wife do? Litigation is surely of no benefit to anyone and amounts to vented anger — unless the money is desperately needed, but it could be wrong to do nothing. Perhaps the appropriate thing would be a letter of thanks for the care that was given along with a strong request for the shortcomings to be investigated and put right.

It is always possible that unscrupulous officials and others may take advantage of us if we are submissive and fail to insist on our rights. In that case we may have to remonstrate with them, or better still, to ask a relative or friend to do so on our behalf. Difficult as it sometimes is, we must still try to remain pleasant and polite.

Our newspapers are full of stories about people claiming compensation from firms, hospitals, airlines and others for some loss or inconvenience they have suffered. It seems as though litigation is a distinctive mark of modern life. Certainly there are plenty of lawyers around who specialise in alerting people to the possibility of claiming large sums of money. It may be right for Christians to involve themselves in such proceedings, but this should be very much a last resort and with sincere regret. Our Lord taught his disciples

> 'blessed are the meek, for they will inherit the earth' (Matthew 5:5),

on which Dr. D. M. Lloyd-Jones comments:

'We are to leave everything, ourselves, our rights, our cause, our whole future in the hands of God, and especially ... if we feel we are suffering unjustly ... you leave yourself and your cause, and your rights and everything with God, with a quietness in spirit and in mind and heart' (*Sermon on the Mount*).

CHAPTER TWENTY TWO

Dreaming Dreams

'There's nothing to live for now, I've only got my memories'. Those are the kind of thoughts that older people can have at times when they are down and depressed. 'What is the world coming to?', we ask, meaning 'it's not like the old days'. It's terribly easy for us to develop this kind of mind-set and not only make ourselves miserable, but also to become very boring to children and any younger people who may be around us. They are not drawn to 'wet blankets' and, to be honest, pessimists are a rather poor witness to the gospel we profess. Family and church life are always enriched by older people who look forward hopefully, rather than backward to the past.

I do not mean that we must blot out the past altogether. Aged people have a story to tell about God's faithfulness over many years, and can bring their experience to bear on the present situation. The problem arises when we give the impression that the past was all good and that the modern generation has little or no worthwhile future. The Bible warns us about this:

> 'Do not say "Why were the old days better than these?"
> For it is not wise to ask such questions' (Ecclesiastes 7:10).

This means that it is foolish for anyone to give the impression that the past was wholly good, with no faults or failings, and that the present is wholly bad and therefore the future is without hope. A wise person, taught by Scripture, knows that such thinking is futile and contrary to the facts.

We need to maintain our zeal for the Lord and his kingdom,

and an attitude of mind and heart that is shaped by the fact that in Christ we are on the victory side. According to the apostle Peter, on the day of Pentecost, an evidence of being filled with the Holy Spirit is

> 'your old men will dream dreams' (Acts 2:17),

which surely means that they will anticipate the Lord's future blessings as great, if not greater, than in the past. Paul had similar thoughts in different words:

> 'We do not lose heart. Though outwardly we are wasting away, yet inwardly we are being renewed day by day' (2 Corinthians 4:16).

In other words, he did not allow the restrictions and discomforts of age to hinder his spiritual growth, and his confidence in the Lord that in the future, his kingdom would grow rather than be diminished.

In his book *The Bumps are what you climb on*, Warren W. Wiersbe draws attention to an Old Testament example (Joshua 14:6-14). 'Caleb is a man who teaches us to look ahead and not back. When the nation of Israel finally did enter the promised land, Caleb could have sat down and pouted. He could have reminded the rulers that he had been in the minority — he had voted to enter the land — and had been right. He could have reviewed those forty years of wasted wandering and complained about them. But he didn't! Instead of looking back, Caleb looked ahead and claimed his mountain.' A New Testament example to inspire us is the aged Simeon, who when he saw the baby Jesus, took him in his arms saying,

> 'Sovereign Lord, as you have promised, you now dismiss your servant in peace. For my eyes have seen your salvation, which you have prepared in the sight of all people, a light for revelation to the Gentiles, and for glory to your people Israel' (Luke 2:29-32).

As we read our daily papers, and see the television news, and as we feel the grip of corruption in society becoming more and more pervasive, we can be forgiven for waves of pessimism coming over us. But we must not let that be our predominant attitude. We know that the Lord is in control and that he is working out his plan which will climax in the personal return of Jesus Christ.

In the providence of God, we senior citizens are advancing in years at a time when the churches in our country are in a low state and there is tremendous confusion even among evangelical churches, with very little evidence of the Holy Spirit at work among us. Again, we have good reason to be concerned about the situation and to have some foreboding about the future. But we must not join the ranks of those who forecast the end of Christian witness in our land. We must remind ourselves of the accounts of the many times in the past when the churches were so corrupt and spiritually impoverished that recovery seemed impossible. At such times, God has brought about amazing transformations. Let us remember that the situation before the great Reformation in the sixteenth century, or before the time of the Wesleys and Whitefield, was considerably worse than anything we have seen. History teaches us that we must never despair, but always encourage ourselves with the words of Jesus,

> 'I will build my church, and the gates of Hades will not overcome it' (Matthew 16:18).

The spiritual condition of the world before Jesus Christ came is described as 'darkness covers the earth and thick darkness is over the peoples' (Isaiah 60:2), and that prophecy continues 'but the LORD rises upon you and his glory appears over you.' That is why a few faithful ones including the aged Simeon, never gave up hope that God's time would come.

Even as we think of ourselves, perhaps with increasing limitations and aggravations of age, we are in a position to have a positive attitude to the future. With the apostle Paul we can say that

> 'our present sufferings are not worth comparing with the glory that will be revealed in us' (Romans 8:18).

The story is told of a Christian of a past century, who, having been told that he only had hours to live, was so thrilled at the prospect of going to glory, that his physical state improved, and as a result, he lived some weeks longer than was anticipated!

When Joseph died in Egypt, he left instructions that his remains were not to be permanently buried in Egypt but in the promised land (Genesis 50:25-26; Hebrews 11:22; Joshua 24:32). He had no option but to leave his family his bones but with them he left a clear message of hope and confidence in the fulfilment of God's promise.

Let us ask the Lord to enable us to sustain a spirit of hopefulness and optimism in the light of the Proverb:

> 'The path of the righteous is like the first gleam of dawn, shining every brighter till the full light of day' (Proverbs 4:18).

CHAPTER TWENTY THREE

Where Are My Glasses?

Don Carson tells the story of Bishop Stanway who was used by God in the outreach of the gospel throughout East Africa, so much so, that some have called him the apostle to Tanzania. Carson writes that 'when I met him, he had returned to his native Australia, and Parkinson's Disease had so debilitated him that he could no longer talk ... By the time I got to know him a little, I felt emboldened to ask him how he was coping with his crippling disease. He had been so active and productive throughout his life: how was he handling being shunted aside? He had to print his answer on a pad of paper three times before I could read it: "there is no future in frustration."'

Let that story prepare us to think about the situation that older folk tend to dread most: it is the condition in which they cannot help themselves. Physical weakness or some disease may rob them of their strength and leave them dependent on others for help in dressing, feeding and other normal functions. It is a good idea to try to imagine ourselves in a situation like that, not to make us fearful or morbid, but to develop a right frame of mind in which to cope with it, if it should happen to us.

Many people say that they are not frightened of death so much as the thought of suffering a long and feeble old age. It is difficult to be willing to enter a second childhood in which one loses one's adult dignity and is stripped of all one's prayerfully acquired knowledge, and has to begin all over again at the mercy of other people.

Perhaps the first thing is to remind ourselves that this world in every aspect is distorted, affected in every part by the invasion of sin. This means that suffering and death are normal in such a world and that people in the conditions we have described are not being singled out for special treatment, much less for special punishment. If we remember this, it will help us to accept our situation and not fight against it. In the Bible, not only do we read about people who reached this stage of helplessness, but in one place it is portrayed for us in graphic poetry (Ecclesiastes 12:1-5). Not all the details in this passage can be identified for certain, but as we briefly look at it, we can recognise some of them:

Verse 2 The picture is of the gradual onset of dusk as the lights are obscured by cloud and fade at last into darkness. So our physical pleasures gradually diminish and a sense of desolation broods over life.

Verses 3-4 The picture now is of a stately home that has seen better days, showing all the signs of decay and deterioration. So our eyes, ears and teeth gradually become the worse for wear, and the once straight back resembles the road sign for 'Beware, elderly crossing', and the voice begins to croak.

Verse 5 Finally, the once firm tread and fearless movement gives way to a hesitant, timid feeling of the way, and inch by inch dragging the body along.

It is a familiar picture, but why is it given to us? The writer concludes his description of old age and death with 'Meaningless! Meaningless! ... Everything is meaningless' and this seems to suggest that a state of helplessness and death itself are hopeless and futile. If this were the case it would leave us simply as objects of pity with nothing to relieve the gloom and misery. Some dear friends have come to that conclusion and see no other way but to end their suffering by taking their own lives. But the writer is not saying that — he is contemplating old age, deliberately leaving God out of the reckoning. Without him all is without hope or purpose, but with him there is meaning and light even in the most helpless state of apparent uselessness. You may be inclined to question that, if so consider another Don Carson illustration:

'Martyn Lloyd-Jones was one of the most influential preachers of the twentieth century. A few weeks before he died, someone asked him how, after decades of fruitful ministry and extraordinary activity, he was coping now he was suffering such weakness it took much of his energy to move from his bed to his armchair and back. He replied in the words of Luke 10:20,

> 'Do not rejoice that the spirits submit to you, but rejoice that your names are written in heaven', adding 'I am perfectly content.'

Such an attitude is the fruit of a mind that has been accustomed in earlier years to think about God, and to meditate on all the benefits that are ours in the Lord Jesus Christ. Those benefits are ours quite independently of our outward circumstances or our physical state. They can be enjoyed even when our situation is unpleasant or we are assailed by pain or discomfort.

In each stage of life a particular aspect of the glory of God becomes especially meaningful to us. So it is that when we are subject to the loss of our physical powers, we can better appreciate that our God is ageless and that his powers are always at 'concert pitch', and we sing:

> Change and decay in all around I see.
> O Thou who changest not, abide with me.
>
> (Henry F. Lyte)

One elderly lady was asked how she coped with her increasing aches and pains. She replied 'Well, I try to keep going, and that is the time when I think I pray more than ever for a bit of comfort when the pain is very bad'. So, did the pain go away then? 'Well, I seem to get comfort — if it hasn't vanished, it seems to ease — the pain is there but still it seems as if you're helped to bear it better.' That is what the Lord promised,

> '... your strength will be equal to your days' (Deuteronomy 33:25).

There are other lessons that come home to us with more meaning than before we began to suffer. For example, our physical weakness makes us very dependent on other people. This has always been the case because never at any stage in life are we entirely independent, but now we realise this more keenly than when we were fit and well. The same is true spiritually, and in our bodily weakness we can reflect on our total dependence on the Lord for every blessing in life. Not only so, as we reach the end of our days on earth it is good to put ourselves completely in his hands and rely on him for our safe transit to glory.

Furthermore our feelings of helplessness in advancing age can lead us to respond to Peter's exhortation:

> 'Dear friends, do not be surprised at the painful trial you are suffering, as though something strange were happening to you. But rejoice that you participate in the sufferings of Christ, so that you may be overjoyed when his glory is revealed' (1 Peter 4:12-13).

It is true that Peter had in mind more especially people who were suffering persecution for their faith, but these words can quite properly be taken to heart by those whose bodies are decaying. They can enter into the sufferings our Saviour endured voluntarily and willingly on their behalf. Think of some of the descriptions we are given of our Lord's sufferings:

> '... there is no one to help' (Psalm 22:11).
>
> 'I am poured out like water, and all my bones are out of joint' (Psalm 22:14).
>
> ' ... there were many who were appalled at him — his appearance was so disfigured beyond that of any man and his form marred beyond human likeness' (Isaiah 52:14).
>
> 'Jesus said, "I am thirsty"' (John 19: 28).

The ravages of age on our bodies are often ugly to see and distressing to bear, both for those who suffer and the loved ones who share in it. But even in this extremity the Lord has given us rays of light, and one of these is a greater sense of thankfulness than ever before that our Lord so loved us, unworthy though we are, that he endured such devastation and desolation for us.

Over and above everything else our reaction to the decay of our bodies and all that goes with it, should be controlled by the fact that one day, these bodies will be restored to perfection. For

> ' ... the Lord Jesus Christ, who, by the power that enables him to bring everything under his control, will transform our lowly bodies so that they will be like his glorious body' (Philippians 3:21).

CHAPTER TWENTY FOUR

Too Much Of A Good Thing?

Among all the miserable and horrible stories you read and hear about, I wonder which causes you the greatest distress? For my part, the kind of tragedy that makes me feel sick is a report of people who have been married for many years, now in retirement, getting divorced. They have the opportunity of enjoying one another's company as never before, and yet it is now that they want to part. This is very sad indeed, but it happens, so alas, this book would not be complete if we failed to ask ourselves why it happens, and what we can do to prevent it.

Before retirement husbands and wives are normally separated for much of the time by the demands of their daily work. Even when the weekend arrives and they welcome the chance to do things together, they may have personal interests that limit that opportunity. Then, suddenly, at retirement they are together day in and day out and their relationship can take on an entirely different shape. In most cases, happily, this means a deepening of their appreciation of one another, and a strengthening of their mutual affection. They discover qualities in their partner they had not seen before, and they enjoy doing things together in the home or in other areas of common interest.

But it does not always work out like that, and instead of a blossoming of love and appreciation, hidden causes of irritation begin to surface that now have every opportunity to become divisive and destructive. Busy lives in previous years have obscured faults and weaknesses, and perhaps even a lack of depth in the partnership. Now they are together for long periods of time, these things can no longer be hidden or suppressed. The problems may be character defects, irritating habits, differences of interests or other niggles of a more or less serious nature.

A major cause of marital breakdown at any stage is an unreasonable expectation of near perfection by one partner of the other. With the longer time spent together in retirement, our imperfections are more and more obvious, in fact, as we grow older, our worst characteristics seem to grow stronger rather than weaker. To be forewarned is to be forearmed — if we are aware of the possible causes of disharmony, with the Lord's help, we can make sure they don't intrude in our relationship.

A possible cause of difficulty with advancing years is a wide difference in the age of married couples. As bodily weakness begins to overtake the older partner, the younger may still be fit for vigorous activity. They always knew the time would come when this would happen, but when it does, it is not always easy to come to terms with it, and it makes tremendous demands on their understanding and tolerance.

There is also the strain caused on a marriage when one partner develops physical problems that demand constant care and attention. Not all of us are born nurses and many a spouse finds this kind of situation more stressful than they can bear. We will consider this more closely in the next chapter.

Another awkward situation is where only one partner is a Christian. This again is much more acute in retirement. Differences in interest show themselves in what they want to do together, and in such things as the kind of television programmes they watch. When a wife is the Christian believer, while her husband has been at work during the week, she has been able to be involved, at least, in daytime church activities. But now he is retired, and he wants her company and resents her wanting to continue as she did before.

For two Christians to separate and divorce at any age, is a great tragedy, but when a marriage breaks up after thirty or forty years or more, it is a first-class disaster. The pain given to the family in such failures is bad enough, but when we add to that the loss to the church and to the world of an example of the sustaining grace of Christ, then we can only weep in despair. This is not to stand in judgement on others or to underestimate the strain some people endure in keeping a marriage intact. But positively, there is scarcely a greater blessing all round, or honour to Jesus Christ, than a Christian couple still in love even as the wrinkles spread and the effects of age, illness or disease, test that love to the limit. Paul's great hymn about love is more than beautiful poetry. It is a challenge to prove what is possible when both partners are yielded to Jesus Christ.

> 'Love is patient, love is kind. It does not envy, it does not boast, it is not proud. It is not rude, it is not self-seeking, it is not easily angered, it keeps no record of wrongs ... always perseveres' (1 Corinthians 13:4-7).

If a marriage is suffering serious tension, it is not only love that is being tested, but our understanding of the Christian life is also under examination. Christians are in danger of allowing the prevailing attitudes in society to affect them, so that what is acceptable is whatever gives us fulfilment. Consequently, if we no longer feel fulfilled in our marriage, then we think we are justified in falling out of it and looking elsewhere. But the life of a Christian as described in the Bible, is almost the exact opposite: for example, our Lord tells us that even he did not please himself but that he sought in every way to please the Father (John 5:30), and the apostle Paul wrote that 'we make it our goal to please him (the Lord)' no matter what our situation might be (2 Corinthians 5:9).

Then, the Bible reminds us that if we are finding life difficult, this is our opportunity to grow in faith and in Christlike character (Romans 5:3-5). It is in this way that we find our fulfilment, and it is in obedience that we prove God's grace to be sufficient for our need. In these days of easy separation and divorce, a Christian example of cheerful faithfulness is of tremendous value.

When a couple begin to realise that they're getting on one another's nerves, they should not allow this to fester. They should talk to each other about it, openly and lovingly. This should lead to praying over it together, asking the Lord for his wisdom and his help. It might even be worth while to share the problem with a pastor or trusted friend. Maybe it is not too late to do more things together either for their own pleasure, or, better still, in some form of help to neighbours or in the church. In this way a potential tragedy can be turned into positive good and the Lord will have the glory.

CHAPTER TWENTY FIVE

For Better, For … ?

Who can forget their wedding day? The weather, the bridesmaids, the service, the tricks some people played on us, the honeymoon. Perhaps a photograph reminds us of the fresh beauty of our bride, or the upright strength of the man we loved. Wonderful!

We always knew it couldn't last and that grey hairs and wrinkles would eventually tell their tale. Down the years there have been times when one has had to nurse the other, for shorter or longer periods. When that happened, we probably reminded one another that we promised to stay the course 'for better for worse, for richer for poorer, in sickness and in health … ' One widower recently told me all about the things he did for his wife who died with cancer. He said, 'I didn't mind that, she was my wife, that's what you do, isn't it?'

We mentioned this briefly in the last chapter, but here we want to explore one of the most distressing situations of all. What happens is this: the husband or wife gradually becomes more and more confused and this can be most bewildering for the partner who is watching it happen. There are a number of reasons why an elderly person may become confused. It is important that any confusion is checked out by a doctor, because it could be caused by something as simple as urine infection. But it may be diagnosed as dementia, and this is not at all easy to cope with.

The following comments may be helpful. They are based on notes kindly made available to me, by a lady whose father looked after his wife who suffered in this way at home for many years. Our friend describes some of the early symptoms that might be present at the onset of dementia:

'The person you thought you knew well begins to mysteriously change. Many things which were part of the daily routine he/she now has difficulty with, or cannot cope with any longer. The relative becomes restless, forgetful, starts to wander, becomes a danger to himself/herself, cannot be left alone, speech becomes unintelligible, cannot hold one-to-one conversations, their personality changes — may become aggressive.'

Carers find their life style changing radically. People suffering from dementia can no longer manage visits to doctors/hospital specialists/nurses/chiropodist/hairdresser on their own; they now need to be accompanied. Personal care of the loved one — washing, feeding, toileting, dressing, medication — have to be fitted into each day as well as cooking/household chores etc. Meal times become increasingly protracted.

Not surprisingly, all this, with the burden of twenty-four hours commitment, has its effect on the physical and emotional well being of the partner. Sometimes this is made worse by feelings of loneliness because relatives or friends stay away, for fear they will be 'out of their depth'. This is one reason, among others, why the caring partner needs to be willing to ask for help and to receive it when it is offered. Such help may include the sharing of household chores or 'sitting in' to give the partner a break, opportunity to go to church or to the shops or to keep other appointments. We should not feel guilty if we have to commit our loved one to someone else's care, because this may well be the best and most loving thing that we can do.

If the sick loved one is a Christian, this is a source of the greatest comfort and a constant reminder that not even dementia can separate anyone from God's love. He or she may not be able to worship, or share in fellowship as before, but the Lord does not expect the impossible, and his love will not waver. In his time, he will take our dear one and make him or her completely whole again.

In these days, there is advice available for those trying to cope with this situation. A doctor or pastor will be able to put them in touch with sources of such help. Up-to-date experience is valuable, and our friend, whom we have already quoted, offers some useful suggestions. For example, we should include people with dementia, as far as possible, in what we are doing, such as letting them watch us at work. We should encourage them to do simple jobs — tasks they used to do regularly they may still be able to undertake, like peeling vegetables or knitting. When speaking to them, it is best for us to sit so they can look directly at us, and to address them regularly by their Christian name. We must try to let them feel loved and wanted by holding their hand, smiling and showing affection regularly. Another thing is to keep them stimulated, perhaps by letting them look at easy to read books, magazines full of pictures, or to read to them following the words with our finger. They may not be able to express themselves very well verbally, but they understand more than we may realise. They will enjoy listening to well known hymns and being sung to, and looking at photographs of the family they can relate to. As the dementia progresses, they will increasingly revert back to the ways of a young child, so why not help them to do very simple children's games, such as jigsaws, or holding soft toys? But be sure there is nothing they can swallow, or harm them in any way. Towards the end of their earthly life, they may become very frail, have difficulty eating, drinking and walking, they will sleep a great deal and lack confidence. As this happens, let us try to reassure them as much as possible. When opportunity arises, it is helpful to read the Bible, pray with them and talk to them about Heaven. To reflect often upon eternity will give us strength and comfort too when the time comes for our loved one to be taken to a better Home.

What we have said here about care for a loved one with dementia, could be applied to other situations, and such things are a big test of our love and faithfulness. The vows we made on our wedding day, were not just part of an empty ritual, and in times like those we are considering here, we can and must look to the Lord before whom we made those vows, to help us to be true to them.

Even more distressing and testing is when a partner loses all recognition of husband or wife. An example would be a colleague who visited his wife in hospital each day for many years, during which time she had no idea who he was. His love for her forbade that he would neglect her, but in his daily visit he needed the Lord's daily strength to endure the pain.

But this is also a challenge to us in days of healthy body and mind. This is the time to commit ourselves to Jesus Christ as our Lord and Saviour — for we can never be sure if and when, we will be too feeble or too muddled to think clearly about the gospel. The subject of this chapter makes it absolutely vital that we should settle our relationship with God without delay, and also that others should know that we are at peace with Him. It might even be a good idea to write an account of your spiritual experience to put with your will (see also chapter 27). Then our loved ones will have something to assure them of our security in Jesus Christ at a time when it will be of the greatest comfort to them.

CHAPTER TWENTY SIX

Unthinkable?

'They just want to get rid of me.' 'I'll go there to die.' 'I don't want to give up my independence.' 'It feels like the end.'

Most pastors, at some time or another, have been on the receiving end of such heart-rending outcries, when it has been suggested that perhaps a retirement home with residential or nursing care should be considered. There are variations on the theme such as 'I can look after myself, I'm not exactly helpless' or 'I have plenty of friends who help me, so I don't need to give up my home.' Resistance like this is perfectly natural and understandable. It is not true of all elderly people because some do take the change calmly and happily, but what can we say to help those who find the whole idea unthinkable?

As you face this question of your future, with all its emotions and complications, let me try to be very practical. Happily, in these days, there are a number of solutions that we might call 'half-way houses' — ways in which we can preserve our independence, at least for a while longer. There are some arrangements we can make that mean we can stay in our own home, but with various kinds of help, so I will mention them first.

Perhaps you are able to look after yourself reasonably well with the help of relatives or friends, but the problem is that you might need help because you feel unwell, or you have fallen down, at a time when no-one is about. The answer could be for you to become linked with one of the community alarm systems so that, in an emergency, you can call for help by simply pressing a button.

But suppose, while you can look after yourself well enough,

your partner is for some reason difficult to care for. In this case you could get relief by arranging for him or her to be taken regularly to a Day Centre. But this may not be enough because your loved one may need more care than can be given at a Day Centre. If this is so, it may be possible for him or her to live in a residential home and to visit you in your own home during the day. In the worst case, it may be your partner will have to be in a residential care home permanently and you would do the visiting. It will not be easy to hand over the responsibility of caring for your partner, but you must not think of this as a failure, rather, thank God that such help is available.

These are just some of the ways by which you can retain your own home base. But maybe your health and situation are such that you really cannot maintain your home, and yet it is not necessary for you to go into residential or nursing care. In that case there are a number of other possibilities you might consider. What I mean is, accommodation with help or care provided, or even meals to save you from cooking. These go by various names, sheltered housing, sheltered accommodation, assisted living, extra care housing etc. These do involve a move but would preserve your independence as far as it is possible. It would be wise for a married couple to consider one or other of these provisions, because it is not easy for a couple to live in residential care where the level of privacy may not be like their own home. You will need to consult people who have experience in these matters, to help you come to a decision.

As we consider these practical questions, and the possibility of losing our independence, let us remind ourselves how the Lord has been with us and helped us in all the changes we have experienced in life until now. We have proved his faithfulness again and again despite all anxieties and fears. If we try to remember all the Lord has been to us since we became Christians, at the very least this will help us to think clearly. We need to ask the Lord to help us to be honest about the advantages and disadvantages of giving up our home and to make us willing to move if that is clearly the right thing to do.

Much depends on our past experience. Some of us will have moved about so many times during our life time that another upheaval is not so daunting for us. Others have lived in the same house for thirty, forty or more years and for them the prospect of moving is like launching into the unknown, both in terms of the move itself and of a future in a community.

At the heart of the problem is a natural distaste for the idea of breaking up a home that contains so much of one's life, so many precious memories, so many things of sentimental value. Most often we will be able to take a few of our precious things with us, so we have at least some to keep our memories alive. But the question remains, how can we cope with this? The feelings are real and not easily dismissed, they are understandable and not to be despised.

As Christians we must try to apply spiritual principles to this problem as we do to any other. We will remember that our heavenly Father knows about it, he loves us and cares for us. Then, very gently and tenderly, I have to ask anyone in this situation whether Christians who are on the way to glory very soon should hold on so tightly to things that belong to this life. People who are not Christians have nothing else to hold on to, but our treasure is in heaven, isn't it? If we begin to think like that, it will help us to think clearly about whether or not to give up our home.

One friend, whose wife and he were over 80 years old when they moved into residential care says 'I think I would advise people not to seek residential care too soon — maintain your independence as long as possible.' Before that encourages you to stay put without further thought our friend goes on to say, 'but on the other hand don't make an idol of your independence and eventually end up a burden to yourself and to others.' That is a wonderfully balanced comment and it sums up the problem; we still have to make a decision one way or the other.

I take it for granted that we commit the matter to the Lord and that we try to be willing to do what is right. Then we need to listen carefully to what our family may have to say, and to consult our pastor or other spiritually minded friend. This does not mean that we should automatically follow the advice we receive, but if both family and spiritual advisers agree in what they say, this surely should go a long way in helping us to make up our minds.

A very important question we must try to answer honestly is whether we are really coping as we say we are. Is our health really good enough for us to look after ourselves and our home properly? Are we as careful as we should be about our personal cleanliness? Is the home we love so well, becoming steadily uncared for? It is easy to say yes to these questions because we don't like to admit the truth! O dear — that's hard, I'm sorry!

Another thing to be careful about, is the willingness of family, neighbours and friends to help us. Sometimes they are so kind that we come to rely on them more and more. They do not complain, and assure us that they are very happy to continue with their help, and that there is no need for us to give up our home because they will look after us. All this is very good for us, and it gives an opportunity for our church or community to express their love in a caring and a practical way. It may well be right for us to accept this situation, but let us be careful not to presume upon it. Let us ask ourselves if we are being unreasonably demanding. As time goes on, our friends will be obliged to do more and more for us; they will do it willingly, but the question is whether it is right for us to allow them to do so. It is not easy to answer such questions, but it is important for us to bear them in mind.

Sometimes the decision as to whether to move is made for us, because our health or circumstances leave us no alternative but to submit. When this happens, we may be sad about it, but we surely must believe that our heavenly Father has over-ruled our situation, and has kindly provided for our need. We will be in the hands of those who are committed to caring for people like us and who are determined to do what is best for us.

With all these things in mind, let's not consider the possibility of giving up our home so unthinkable after all.

CHAPTER TWENTY SEVEN

Thinkable!

Well, willingly or reluctantly you have decided to go into residential care, so now, go for it! Make up your mind that you are going to enjoy this new provision the Lord has made for you, and there is no reason why you should not do so. The best thing now is to prepare yourself for the new kind of life you are about to begin.

Despite all the change and upheaval there will be some things that will remain obstinately the same. We will still be imperfect people living among imperfect people. If we ever had the notion that a Christian retirement home is the next thing to heaven on earth, alas, we will be sadly disillusioned. Don't misunderstand me. Of course, living with Christian people will be wonderful as you share together in spiritual blessing, and enjoy fun together without sinful and corrupting influences. What a lovely way to enter the last phase of our life on earth! But let us prepare ourselves for the fact that there may be boring people to cope with, people who try to dominate every conversation, those who hate losing at Scrabble and even those whose habits are offensive. We may be tempted to lose patience with other residents, until we remember that they more than likely find us also very irritating. What a wonderful setting in which to bring forth the fruit of the Spirit!

> '... love, joy, peace, patience, kindness, goodness, faithfulness, gentleness and self-control' (Galatians 5:22-23).

As time goes by you will discover those with whom you can form a closer friendship to make up for the loss of fellowship with friends in your own church. It is surprising how refreshing that can be.

Perhaps one of the things that put you off the idea of going into a home was the thought of being regimented or forced into a routine. This is not as bad as some people say it is, but, let us face the fact that in any home there has to be some kind of routine and it follows that the more residents there are, the more obvious will be the need for order in daily life and conduct. For most of the time there will be personal liberty, but a community has to be structured and the absence of good organisation never did lead to greater happiness anywhere, but only greater burdens on the caring staff.

This is a new way of life that we will better enjoy if we have in mind some guidelines I have culled from notes kindly sent me by an experienced worker in this field.

One of the first things with which we would need to come to terms is the fact that we would be living closely with people in all kinds of physical condition. Some will show few signs of age, but others may be handicapped and still others may be mentally confused. If we are not careful, we could develop feelings of revulsion, or we could despise such people. We will need to banish those feelings, and to replace them with sympathy and helpfulness, and to be very thankful for our own good state of health.

Then we must beware of boring other residents with our constant talk about our church. We may want to tell them how good it is, or we may be full of complaints about it. Our new friends will want to know about where we have worshipped and served the Lord in the past, and share our prayers and concerns, but we must not over-burden them with our interests, and we must also be careful to share in theirs.

Another thing to remember is that the staff will almost certainly be over-worked, so we must try to be patient with them, if they're not always cheerful or if they fail to do immediately what we expect. It is all too easy to develop a complaining, critical attitude that does not help the situation, and in any case, is very wrong for Christians to adopt.

There will be lots of opportunities to discuss ideas of all kinds with other residents; that is one of the great benefits of going into a care residential situation. But be sure you listen to others and that you are not dogmatic or domineering when you air your views.

You will receive a great deal of advice about your move out and your move into the home, and it will be sensible to heed that advice especially when it comes from those who have experience in seeing people through this radical change in their lives. For example, a decision has to be made about how much of your own furniture you can take with you. This is a terribly painful part of the process, but it is really very important to try not to take more than the home recommends. We have to grit our teeth with this one and be prepared to lose many precious items but hold in our minds the memories they evoke.

Not long ago I was visiting a relative in the large lounge of a secular retirement home. One of the staff politely interrupted the TV viewing and general buzz of conversation to introduce two young women who, she said, would teach them some games to add some interest to their lives. The response from thirty or forty stony faces was an equally stony silence, except that I distinctly heard one uncompromising female voice 'over my dead body'! Perhaps communal games are not the best way of developing a community spirit and we would not want organised events so to dominate that there is no room for personal choice. But it would be very strange indeed in a Christian home if nothing were done to bring residents together.

Staff in such homes will have an eye to the mental and physical exercise necessary for our well being. So we will be prepared at times to be urged to bestir ourselves to some activity with others when we might prefer to be left alone. We will be glad that we allowed ourselves to be disturbed, and to co-operate with planned activities, so will everyone else.

Did you think that going into a home would mean that you would no longer have the feeling of being wanted? If you thought like that you were mistaken, because there are all kinds of ways in which you can be helpful. At one home, Harry made himself the 'shopper in chief' for other residents, and waited on visiting ministers making sure the desk was right for them and anything else to make them feel at ease. Whatever skills you have will most probably be useful in your new environment. Here are some examples:

1. You can give general assistance to the staff under their guidance, such as cleaning tables, flower arranging, care of house plants, and even gardening if you are fit enough.

2. Do you have musical skills? Then you can help with the services and give pleasure to the other residents.

3. If you are an artist or are good at handicrafts, there are many ways those gifts can be used, especially when it comes to Open Days, or helping others to develop a skill they never had.

4. Maybe you have been used to leading a women's meeting or some other spiritual ministry in your church. If so, it is more than likely that there is a way you can be used in the home.

5. If you are an outgoing kind of person and love to get alongside others to help and encourage them, then there is certainly a work for you to do in the place to which you are going.

Tell yourself this move is going to turn out for good and you are going to be happy, and ask the Lord to help you make it so.

CHAPTER TWENTY EIGHT

Yet All With Wings!

I have reasonable health, am happily married, and live comfortably in a nice semi-detached bungalow. I have happy memories of earlier years, and I am still able to serve the Lord in limited ways. My children and my grandchildren love me and I love them. In other words, I have good reason to cling to this earthly life.

We naturally cling to life, and this is one of the ways by which God sustains human life on earth. When our health is reasonably good, we are comfortable at home with a measure of security, and our loved ones are around us. Life is good and we are torn between two, as was the apostle Paul:

> 'If I am to go on living in the body, this will mean fruitful labour for me. Yet what shall I choose? I do not know! I am torn between the two: I desire to depart and be with Christ, which is far better; but it is more necessary for you that I remain in the body' (Philippians 1:22-24).

Perhaps then, our health begins to fail and we increasingly lose patience with the world around us, the sordid television programmes, the discordant tones of modern music or the strident utterings of the pop stars. We gradually have sympathy with the old song 'I don't feel at home in this world anymore'. This is God's way of tipping the balance of our desires heavenward, as the hymn expresses it so helpfully:

For Thou, who knowest, Lord, how soon
Our weak heart clings,

Hast given us joys, tender and true,
Yet all with wings,
So that we see, gleaming on high,
Diviner things.

I thank Thee, Lord, that here our souls
Though amply blest,
Can never find, although they seek,
A perfect rest,
Nor ever shall, until they lean
On Jesus' breast.

(Adelaide Annie Proctor 1825-64).

So, when life becomes less bearable, the love of life begins to wane and we become more and more out of sorts with the world with which our grandchildren are learning to cope, let us remember that this is God's way of preparing us for our departure.

Here in the body pent,
Absent from Him I roam,
Yet nightly pitch my moving tent
A day's march nearer home.

(James Montgomery 1771-1854).

One of the realities of the Christian life that we do not think about as much as we should, is that it has some built-in tensions. For example, there is necessarily both trusting and trying in the Christian life: if we trust without trying we will not make progress, and if we try without trusting, we will surely fail. Both trusting and trying are essential to a healthy spiritual experience. As we approach the end of life on earth, we encounter other tensions. On the one hand we look forward to meeting the Lord and serving him forever, and yet we hate the idea of leaving our loved ones.

There is a similar tension as we look forward to the Second Coming of our Lord Jesus Christ. This world is so full of suffering and corruption that we long to see an end to it all. But then we remember loved ones and friends who are not saved, and we are torn in our minds, wanting our Lord to come and yet dreading the consequences if that happens before they are converted.

The question is what should we do with this tension? The first thing is to accept it as normal Christian experience; it is not abnormal and we should not have guilty feelings about it. Secondly, we should try to give equal attention to both sides, treating them like the two ends of violin string. When the tension is right, the string gives the right note and music is possible. So if we give equal stress in our minds to the hope we have in Christ and to the desire we have for the salvation of others, then our lives will be at the right pitch. But as we draw nearer to the end of our lives, we should be prepared for a greater longing for home, and for our minds to be more occupied than ever with the prospect of seeing the Lord in his beauty and splendour. We must prayerfully and deliberately leave our loved ones to the loving and wise purposes of God.

If we are saved, then the glory of heaven will increasingly have greater attraction than anything in life on earth, no matter how pleasant. Our attitude as Christians to the prospect of death, must be seen to be in contrast to those who are without Christ. One example of the attitude of non-Christians, is the saying of John Paul Richter (1763 - 1825): 'what makes old age so sad is not that our joys, but our hopes cease.' What a pity it is that unconverted people settle for that kind of thing when in Christ, their hopes could outlive their joys. Many years ago when some ministers were sharing their thoughts about death, one of them said, 'I have nothing to do with death; my business is to live as long as I can — as well as I can — and to serve my Lord and Master as faithfully as I can, until he shall think proper to call me home.' (W.Tennent Jnr. quoted in The *Log College*, by A.Alexander, Banner Of Truth, 1968).

Now let me be very practical. If we are not afraid of death, we will not hesitate to prepare for it. For example, if you have not made a will, why not do so? This will be a great kindness to your family because it will save them all kinds of problems at a time when they will be grieving for you. Be sure to have your will drawn up by a solicitor. There is really no substitute for this because they know exactly how to word it so as to be sure your loved ones will have no problems.

Along with making a will, it is also a good idea to appoint someone to look after your affairs at such a time as you may not be able to cope with them yourself. For example, suppose you had a stroke and you could not think or speak clearly, then someone would need to handle your finances, but this would be very difficult, unless you had named someone in advance. This is called arranging an enduring power of attorney and needs to be done on an official form. (See details at the end of the book).

Another very practical matter is including in your will some ideas about your funeral service — suggest hymns and Bible readings and anything else to help those who will arrange the service. Make sure that what you ask for reflects the certainty of our faith to lift the hearts of Christian friends and to challenge unconverted relatives and others who will be there. It is also most helpful if you indicate your wishes about burial or cremation, or if you are not concerned either way. And then it is a good idea to say whether or not you give permission for organs of your body to be donated for the benefit of others.

An important preparation for our departure is to make sure, so far as we can, that we are not only at peace with God, but also with all who know us. If there is a rift that needs repairing, forgiveness to be asked for or offered, let us deal with these things before it is too late.

The most important thing of all is to leave your family and friends in no doubt about your spiritual state. No matter whether you leave much or little of material worth, the best legacy of all is the assurance of your faith in the Lord Jesus Christ as your Saviour from sin and its consequences. This will make all the difference to the atmosphere at your funeral and the feelings of those who mourn for you. This is especially desirable if for any reason you have never declared your faith publicly in believer's baptism or some other way. Secret disciples leave uncertainty in the minds of those who mourn their passing, which is very sad and can be avoided if only they will make a simple statement in their will or some other place.

Richard Baxter (1615-1691) put the right attitude of Christians to the approach of death into a simple verse:

If life be long, I will be glad
That I may long obey;
If short, yet why should I be sad
To soar to endless day?

CHAPTER TWENTY NINE

Lost Awhile

At 11 o'clock one November Sunday night, my wife Muriel went to be with the Lord. One moment she was saying how she had enjoyed the services at the church that day and felt really good, the next moment she was gone, as sudden as switching off a light.

It is difficult to describe our feelings when the parting comes or to understand our reactions. Nothing in the past seems to prepare us for the inner sense of desolation. But the reality is that the older we grow, the greater is the possibility that loved ones and friends will go ahead of us into eternity. When this happens we can confirm the Psalmist's testimony:

> 'Even though I walk through the valley of the shadow of death, I will fear no evil, for you are with me; your rod and your staff, they comfort me' (Psalm 23:4).

Perhaps our loss has been a wife or husband, a brother or sister, mother or father, or some other close relative or dear friend. In any case, the feeling is as though we ourselves are in 'the shadow of death', and it is then that we are comforted if we have been accustomed to turning to the Lord in times of need.

The first and most important thing to remember in connection with bereavement, is the need to grieve and to allow our grief to take its natural course. Donald Howard says:

'A major problem is that we are too fearful of showing emotion: "boys don't cry". Why shouldn't they? When Jesus wept at the grave of his friend Lazarus, more than mere emotion was being expressed, but he *did* weep. God gave us our emotions and we are foolish to ignore them. Rather than tears indicating a so-called nervous breakdown, they are often a safety valve to reduce the pressure that might otherwise cause a collapse.'

We all have different personalities and temperaments and nowhere is this more clearly demonstrated than in our instant reaction to bereavement. Some shed copious tears while others beat the air in bitterness or frustration. Some want to be alone, while others crave for company. Some feel limp and unable to do anything, while others work off their feelings in busyness and perhaps even unnecessary activity.

There may be a difference between our immediate reactions and the long term effects of grievous loss. Some of these may need to be gradually overcome, such as the tendency to constant activity; sooner or later, we need to calm down to a more natural way of life. If we have tended to shun company and to keep ourselves at home, then the time must come when we return to normal social life.

It is quite common for a widow to act as though her husband were still alive, even to the extent of talking to him and asking questions as she would have done before. Don't be embarrassed about that. It may well take quite a time to adjust to his absence. At the same time, we must try to overcome the natural tendency to wish that our loved one was still back with us. We can do this best by constantly reminding ourselves that they are better off with the Lord, and that, in God's good time, we will go to be with them. This is the time to prove, what we may have believed for a long time, that the Lord is with us and will meet our needs.

Another temptation is to self-pity. When we first suffer our loss our friends will gladly listen to our expressions of grief and fears for the future, but as time goes on, if we repeat these things over and over again we will be very likely to lose those friends and that will make our situation worse. It is better by far for us, when the first effects of the shock are fading, to look around to see what we can do to help ourselves or someone else — this is the best known cure for self-pity.

Both my wife Georgie, and I, have lost our first partners. When we began to be drawn together and ultimately to marry, we found that we had both drunk deeply out of the same well — Philippians 4:11-13. We had learned from experience, that the Lord is able to give a real and deep contentment at the point of our pain and grief.

So far, I have assumed that the person we have lost was a believer and that we can therefore, take comfort in his or her happiness in the Lord's presence. But this is not always so, and we sometimes have to bid farewell to those who were not professing Christians or who were even opposed to 'religion' or scoffed at the gospel. This adds immensely to our grief and is very difficult to bear. It would be quite wrong for me to minimise the seriousness of this situation or to offer a spurious comfort to those who bear the burden of such sorrow. Nevertheless, there are two comforting thoughts that, it seems to me, we are right to consider. The first is that it is not for us to read the human heart. We only know the outward appearance and we are not in a postion to judge anyone else's final spiritual state. There may well have been last thoughts of repentance, acceptable to God, of which we are totally unaware.

The second consideration is that we believe in a God who is both just and merciful and we do well to rest our minds where Abraham did long ago

> 'will not the Judge of all the earth do right?' (Genesis 18:25).

If you have prayed for your relative or friend as Abraham did for Lot, then the way of faith is for us also to leave the matter in God's hands.

If we are bereaved, we should try to remember that the friends around us are in an awkward position. They will want to comfort us, to do the right thing, and find the right words. The result is that sometimes they can be tongue tied, or if they speak, their words will sound trite or unreal. We must try to help them and we will certainly not do this by asking people not to talk to us. We must allow them to express their sympathy and love even if it is not easy for them to do so. By far the best way is for us to speak first. For instance, 'how good of you to come'; 'I am so glad to see you'; 'did you have a good journey?'; 'it is good of you to call — you are such a busy person'. This will break the ice and make it easier for well wishers to feel comfortable with us.

It is silly for Christians to try to prove the reality of their faith by being jolly and jovial in a time of bereavement. Christianity was never intended to make us unnatural, and a total absence of genuine grief is unreal. Our simple trust in our heavenly Father will come through in our sober bearing and in our quiet confidence in the gospel of the resurrection.

CHAPTER THIRTY

Second Or Third!

'What a recommendation for marriage,' people say, when a widow or widower re-marries, and so it is! But, like the first time, as the marriage service says: 'it is not to be entered into carelessly, lightly or selfishly — but responsibly, thoughtfully and in the fear of God.'

Muriel and I had been married for over forty years; although she had treatment for a heart problem, neither I nor our family were prepared for the night the Lord took her to himself. It was painless and so sudden that there was no opportunity for any kind of parting word. My family were wonderful, my Christian friends were supportive and I had plenty to occupy my mind in serving the Lord. And yet, though all this is true without question, there was also a feeling of desolation arising from the loss of loving companionship I had enjoyed for so long.

After some months, Georgie came on the scene. In a sense she had been there a long time as a good friend of both Muriel and me. She was a widow, her husband having died some twenty years earlier, and the idea of marrying again began to take shape. But what would other people think? What about our families? Where would we live? And a whole lot of other questions crowded in such as, how could we develop a close friendship without other people drawing conclusions before we were ready ourselves?

I have told our story thus far because there will be those whose experience has been similar to ours and others maybe, who are in the earlier stages and wondering whether to go ahead. This question is made much easier if it has been discussed in advance with our first partner. It is just one of the many blessings that arise out of a relationship that is trusting and open, and all marriages are meant to be like that, especially when the partners are Christians. Almost the first worry that intrudes when re-marrying is contemplated, is whether such a thing would be unfaithful to the one who has died or in some way tarnishing the love that is still warm and genuine towards him or her. If we do not have these thoughts ourselves, we may worry that other people will have them, and despise us for our 'disloyalty' to the departed. All such worries are set aside if in happier times, each partner has told the other to feel free to marry another when one or other is taken. This is liberating and lifts what otherwise can be a heavy burden. It does not mean that we think less of those who feel that their love for their first partner prohibits any thought of another marriage; each person must feel comfortable within, and above all, at peace with the Lord.

It is most important to bear in mind that in re-marrying we do not stop loving one partner in order to begin loving another. Our experience is that our first love remains, and indeed at times surfaces most powerfully. This does not mar the new relationship, but enriches it when both partners share that very experience and they can talk together about it. What I am trying to say is this, companionship is one of God's wonderful gifts, and if after a time of mourning, he opens the way for a new beginning, there is nothing wrong with the idea, but rather it is a perfectly reasonable and sensible thing to do.

Some people will be keen to warn us about being 'caught on the rebound' — that is grasping at a new relationship too early in our grief, without time for adequate reflection. This is a danger to be avoided, especially if the friendship is an entirely new one. We must not rush into re-marriage any less prepared than for our first experience. The problem is not so great if the proposed re-marriage is on the basis of a long term friendship.

In our new found love, we must not be so starry eyed as to ignore possible areas of difficulty. We must consider them seriously, not to be daunted, but to find ways of overcoming them. Wide difference in age is always a matter for serious thought when contemplating marriage, and this is no less necessary in the case of second marriages. Prospective partners who are very much younger than the other, must ask themselves if their love, admiration and mutual interests will be strong enough to face the possible conflicts that may arise because the contrast in their physical state becomes more significant. They may even have to face long periods of caring for the ageing partner. The answer has often been positive and successful, but this should not be taken for granted without prayerful thought.

A situation, also requiring adequate consideration is where one partner of a proposed remarriage has always been single. Such people are bound to be 'set in their ways' and all too often have been unable to adapt to kind of shared life that marriage involves. A marriage of this kind may well succeed, but again, the issues need to be faced honestly, openly and prayerfully before going ahead.

Then there are practical questions such as where to live, and how to combine two homes. Whose car has to go? Whose cooker is the best? Which one snores most! Which pictures shall we retain? How can two lots of finance be merged? It may be we will need advice from a pastor or someone in banking. Some of these areas may be worrying but more than likely, before long, answers will be found.

By far and away the greatest potential difficulty, will most probably be in connection with the families of such new partners. The prospect of a stepfather or mother is not always welcome for many reasons, especially if the new relationship has been unexpected and is suddenly thrust upon them. All kinds of questions arise, and it is important, gently and sensitively, to introduce him or her to them and give them time and space to work out this new and unexpected situation for themselves. In our case, we had both kinds of situation to handle. My family knew Georgie, partly because Muriel often spoke about her, and partly because one son-in-law knew her from earlier acquaintance. Georgie's family had only the slightest idea of what I was like, so it was not easy for them, but by the time of the speeches at the wedding, good relationships had been forged and they happily continue.

Some emotional reaction to the news of a prospective re-marriage can be expected and needs to be respected. Very often the question in the mind of a daughter or son is, 'how can any one take the place of my father, or my mother?' Again, in the enthusiasm of our new found love, and perhaps the desirability for an early wedding, we must bear with these feelings and not trample upon them.

Suspicions can arise as to whether there is some hidden agenda behind the proposed marriage. This can happen especially if one of the new partners has a higher position, or more money than the other. Will the new stepfather or mother cream off the inheritance that would have come to the children?

Circumstances differ very much from family to family, but let us underline that a Christian attitude will ensure that suspicions, irritations and tensions are understood and sympathetically handled, so that the future family relationships are as harmonious as we can make them, with freedom of access and communication all round.

Whatever gave pleasure within the two families before the marriage, should so far as possible, still be accommodated. Let children and grandchildren see no less of their parents and grandparents than before this new home was set up. We must strive to create as little disturbance as possible within the family circle.

While we must do our best to minimise any problems that arise and nullify objections so far as we can, we should not allow other people to dictate our decision. We will listen to what they say and honestly consider any serious argument put to us, but, in the end, the decision is ours.

When Georgie and I were married, it gave us great pleasure to see the smiles that came on people's faces when they knew what was happening; it made so many other people happy to see us together. When one church group were told the news, they all cheered! And that is how it should be!

CHAPTER THIRTY ONE

The Lord Is Coming Again

I know not when my Lord may come;
I know not how, nor where;
If I shall pass the vale of death,
Or meet him in the air.

(D.W. Whittle 1840 - 1901)

Our departure from this life will be by one of two ways, either we will die, or the Lord will return and take us to himself before then. Either way, the prospect is very pleasant! In this chapter, let us imagine that the Lord returns before our life on earth comes to a natural end.

> His coming will be most glorious: 'For the Lord himself will come down from heaven, with a loud command, with the voice of the archangel and with the trumpet call of God, and the dead in Christ will rise first' (1 Thessalonians 4:16).

This has inspired hymn writers like Frances R. Havergal to produce poetry like this:

Thou art coming, O my Saviour,
Thou art coming, O my King,
In Thy beauty all-resplendent,
In Thy glory all-transcendent —
Well may we rejoice and sing:

Coming! in the opening east
Herald brightness slowly swells;
Coming! O my glorious Priest,
Hear we not Thy golden bells?

If we are on earth when Jesus returns some very wonderful things will happen to us. For instance we

> 'will be caught up ... to meet the Lord in the air' (1 Thessalonians 4:17).

What an experience that will be! Perhaps you never thought you might go for a space flight: the very idea scares you because it would be so hazardous, you never know what might go wrong! But if the Lord comes to take you there will be no space rockets, blast-offs, peculiar clothing, oxygen supplies or any such things; he will take you as you are, perfectly prepared and in complete safety.

But that is not all. Paul tells us that all the Lord's people who have died before he comes, will be with the Lord in the air, so we will join them in a grand re-union. It is difficult for us to imagine what this will be like, but we can be sure the whole scene will be one of amazing glory and joy.

The question had arisen in the early church as to whether the believers who died before Jesus returned would lose some blessings that will be enjoyed by those who are still alive on earth at that glorious moment. The answer is clear; there will be no advantage or loss either way. Both those who have gone before and those who are here when Jesus comes will meet together with the Lord at one and the same time sharing those great scenes of jubilation.

Then there will be the glorious resurrection. At the end of chapter 23, we mentioned this as something to help us cope with the pains and troubles of our ageing bodies. In the gospel story, Martha was comforted about her brother Lazarus's death:

> 'I know he will rise again in the resurrection at the last day' (John 11:24).

If doubts assail us about this, then we should once again reflect on the all wise, all powerful God, made known to us in the Bible, whom we worship. We cannot understand how the resurrection will happen, but we do know that nothing is impossible to such a God. This is how the apostle Paul argued:

> ' ... he who raised Christ from the dead will also give life to your mortal bodies through his Spirit who lives in you' (Romans 8:11).

We may want to ask what our resurrection bodies will be like. The only clue the Bible gives us is that they will be similar to our Lord's glorified body (Philippians 3:21). In another place Paul tells us:

> ' ... we will all be changed — in a flash, in the twinkling of an eye, at the last trumpet. For the trumpet will sound, the dead will be raised imperishable, and we will be changed' (1 Corinthians 15: 51-52).

Great as those blessings are, they will be eclipsed by one that outshines them all. Paul tells us:

> 'And so we will be with the Lord for ever' (1 Thessalonians 4:17).

Here is the ultimate blessing that all true believers anticipate with the greatest longing. It is one of the joys our Lord prayed that his disciples would have:

> 'Father, I want those you have given me to be with me where I am, and to see my glory ...' (John 17:24).

O the joy to see Thee reigning,
Thee, my own belovèd Lord!
Every tongue Thy name confessing,
Worship, honour, glory, blessing
Brought to Thee with glad accord —

Thee, my Master and my Friend,
Vindicated and enthroned,
Unto earth's remotest end
Glorified, adored, and owned!

(Frances Ridley Havergal 1836 - 79).

This is the supreme prospect for every Christian. In the midst of life's trials and testings, spiritual conflict and increasing physical weakness, let us encourage ourselves with the great hope of our Lord's return

> '... while we look for the blessed hope — the glorious appearing of our great God and Saviour, Jesus Christ ...' (Titus 2:13).

CHAPTER THIRTY TWO

The Deep River

If the Lord does not come first then we all must pass through the experience of death. Christians, of all people, should be able to think, talk and even sing about death:

So when my latest breath
Shall rend the veil in twain,
By death I shall escape from death,
And life eternal gain.
That resurrection-word,
That shout of victory;
Once more, 'For ever with the Lord!'
Amen, so let it be!

(James Montgomery 1771 - 1854).

It is natural for us to dislike the idea of dying, because it so often involves pain and physical distress. It is surrounded by mystery — we have not been this way before. But Jesus Christ is always the answer to our problems. As we take this road we can remember that he did so before us. For him it was a rougher road than anything we will endure, so his presence with us in this hour of our extremity will be the comfort of one who knows from experience what it is like.

Apart from the anxiety that comes from facing the unknown, the main cause of fear in death is the knowledge of our sinfulness and unworthiness, and Satan loves to bring this before us in our weakness. The answer is to fix our eyes on Jesus and commit ourselves totally to him. This is what Paul had in mind:

> 'The sting of death is sin, and the power of sin is the law. But thanks be to God! He gives us the victory through our Lord Jesus Christ' (1 Corinthians 15: 56-57).

Those who are trusting Jesus Christ for salvation, should have no fear of God's judgement because their sins are forgiven. The sting has been taken out of death.

The circumstances of Jonah's experience were, to say the least, very unusual. When he was inside the big fish he says:

> '... my life was ebbing away'. [What did he do?] 'I remembered you, Lord, and my prayer rose to you, to your holy temple' (Jonah 2:7).

This is even more helpful to us if we recall that at that time, Jonah had disobeyed the Lord and was suffering because of his backsliding. None of this prevented Jonah from praying to God with confidence until he exclaimed:

> 'Salvation comes from the Lord' (Jonah 2:9). [Let this be our assurance, too, as we go] ... 'through the valley of the shadow of death' (Psalm 23:4).

Not only so, there is the positive view, the prospect of heaven is such that we can face the transition with peace because of the joy and glory that await us. It was 'for the joy set before him', that our Lord himself 'endured the cross (Hebrews 12:2), and at the other end of the valley for us is the wonder of sharing that joy with him.

In his great story of a *Pilgrim's Progress*, John Bunyan pictures the experience of death as crossing a river. Christian and his friend Hopeful asked if the water was of equal depth everywhere, and the answer they received was that the depth varied according 'as you believe in the King of the place'. For Hopeful, the water was shallow and he soon found his feet, but poor Christian felt as though he was sinking and began to fear that he would never reach the Celestial City. But as they remembered the promises of God 'they both took courage, and the enemy was, after that, as still as a stone, until they were gone over.'

The lesson from Bunyan is, though some of us are brave and some are timid, and some have stronger faith than others, the Lord will see us through to himself. He will use the comfort and consolation of family and friends, supremely when they remind us of the great promises of God and his everlasting covenant which it is impossible for him to break.

When the Lord calls us home, we are not to think that we have failed if we have feelings of trepidation that are natural to those going where they have not been before. It is a solemn moment in which we know we are leaving behind many tearful hearts. This is natural and faith does not eradicate natural emotions, but at the same time the Lord will enable us to enjoy a sense of entering into the victory our Lord has won for us.

His oath, His cov'nant, and His blood,
Support me in the whelming flood;
When all around my soul gives way,
He then is all my hope and stay.
On Christ, the solid Rock, I stand;
All other ground is sinking sand.

(Edward Mote 1797 - 1874).

CHAPTER THIRTY THREE

The Celestial City

'Oh that will be glory for me,' we sing, and so it will, be sure of that and keep that vision always in your mind.

Don Carson tells the story of a young woman named Florence Chadwick, who attempted to swim the distance between Catalina Island and main land California. Since she had already swum the English Channel both ways, she had every good reason to think that she would succeed. The weather was foggy and chilly and she swam for fifteen hours. By then she was physically and emotionally exhausted and, again and again, she begged to be taken out of the water. But at last, they took her out when she was a mere half a mile from her destination. Afterwards she said, 'I think that if I could have seen the shore I would have made it.'

As we keep our minds fresh with Scripture, we can 'see the shore' and this will give us strength as well as glad anticipation. The prospect is so wonderful that it is described in Scripture by many different pictures such as, a home (John 14:2), a heavenly country (Hebrews 11:16), a city with golden pavements (Hebrews 11:10 and Revelation 21:10-21), a wedding reception (Matthew 25:1-13), and a beautiful garden (Revelation 22:1-3). All these whet our appetite, and whether we are alive when Jesus returns or whether we experience death, if we are trusting in him as our Lord and Saviour, we will in the end be citizens of the new heaven and earth. As the apostle Peter wrote:

> '... in keeping with his promise, we are looking forward to a new heaven and a new earth, the home of righteousness' (2 Peter 3:13).

The world that we know that was made by God and in which he delighted, has been infested by sin and corruption and every part of it is spoiled, bringing pain and disaster. This is the world with which we are familiar, but it is not going to stay like that. When Jesus comes, the whole universe will be purified and every trace of sin and its consequences removed. This is how it was revealed to the apostle John:

> 'Then I saw a new heaven and a new earth, for the first heaven and the first earth had passed away, and there was no longer any sea. I saw the Holy City, the new Jerusalem, coming down out of heaven from God, prepared as a bride beautifully dressed for her husband. And I heard a loud voice from the throne saying, "now the dwelling of God is with men, and he will live with them. They will be his people, and God himself will be with them and be their God. He will wipe every tear from their eyes. There will be no more death or mourning or crying or pain, for the old order of things has passed away"' (Revelation 21:1-4).

When Jesus said to his disciples that the meek would inherit the earth (Matthew 5:5), this is at least part of what he meant.

'... the Bible assures us that God will create a new earth on which we shall live to God's praise in glorified, resurrected bodies. On that new earth, therefore, we hope to spend eternity, enjoying its beauties, exploring its resources, and using its treasures to the glory of God' (A.A.Hoekema, *The Bible and the Future)*.

Once again remember the request made by our Lord in his great prayer in John 17,

> 'Father, I want those you have given me to be with me where I am, and to see my glory ...' (Verse 24).

If we truly love him nothing will please us more than to see him glorified, sharing the Father's throne, as he did before he left it to come to our rescue.

So, why don't we join John Bunyan in his dream about the pilgrim named Christian, and his friend Hopeful, as they approached the Celestial City.

'Now I saw in my dream that these two men went in at the gate; and lo, as they entered, they were transfigured, and they had raiment put on that shone like gold. There were also that met them with harps and crowns, and gave them to them — the harps to praise withal, and the crowns in token of honour. Then I heard in my dream that all the bells in the city rang again for joy, and that it was said unto them, **"Enter ye into the joy of your Lord."** I also heard the men themselves, that they sang with a loud voice, saying, **"blessing, and honour, and glory, and power, be unto him that sitteth upon the throne, and unto the lamb, for ever and ever."**

Now just as the gates were opened to let in the men, I looked in after them, and, behold, the City shone like the sun; the streets also were paved with gold, and in them walked many men, with crowns on their heads, palms in their hands, and golden harps to sing praises withal!

There were also of them that had wings, and they answered one another without intermission, saying, "Holy, holy, holy, is the Lord." And after that, they shut up the gates; which, when I had seen, I wished myself among them.'

O sweet and blesséd country,
The home of God's elect!
O sweet and blesséd country
That eager hearts expect!
Jesus, in mercy bring us
To that dear land of rest,
Who art, with God the Father
And Spirit, ever blest!

(Bernard of Cluny, 12th cent.
tr. by John Mason Neale, 1818-66).

BIBLIOGRAPHY

Christians grieve too	Donald Howard	Banner of Truth
Christians grow old	David Gay	Hughes & Coleman Ltd.
Celebrate Life after 50	Roger Palms	Victor Books
An Age Old Problem	Roger Hitchings	Article in issue 42, B.E.C. 'Foundations' Spring 99.
Who Cares?	Addressed to Carers	Health Education Authority
Caring For The Elderly	Care Action File	Issue eleven.
Christians in Retirement	Michael Botting	Grove Booklets Ltd.
The Bonus Years	John Cansdale	Paternoster Press (1979)
High Time Directory	Christian Vocations	

BOOKS BY THE SAME AUTHOR

Only Servants

Born Slaves

The Beauty of Jesus

Our Father

For Starters

This is our God

USEFUL ADDRESSES

ENDURING ATTORNEY

The Solicitor's Law Society, Oyez House, 7 Spa Road, London, S.E.16 3QQ

PILGRIM HOMES

175, Tower Bridge Road, London, S.E.1 2AL (02074675466)

CARE

Challenge House, 29, Canal Street, Glasgow, G4 OAD (0345 626576)

HELP THE AGED

16-18, St.James Walk, Clerkenwell Green, London, EC IR OBE (02072530253)

AGE CONCERN

Astral House, 1268, London Road, London, SW 16 4ER (020 8679 8000)

WORDS THAT FIT

In times of:-

DOUBT	Romans 8:38-39, Isaiah 49:15-16, Jeremiah 31:3-4, Romans 5:8
WORRY	Isaiah 26:3, Psalm 42:5, 55:22, 1 Peter 5:7
FEAR	Isaiah 41:13, 43:1-2, Psalm 56:3-4, 91:14-16
ILLNESS	Psalm 103:13-14; Romans 8:35, 2 Corinthians 12:9, Hebrews 4:15-16
SLEEPLESSNESS	Psalm 4:8, Numbers 6:24-26, Psalm 62:1, 121:1-8
IMPATIENCE	Colossians 3:12, Proverbs 14:29, 19:11; Galatians 5:22-23
BEREAVEMENT	Deuteronomy 32: 27a, Isaiah 61:1 66:13, 2 Corinthians 1:3-4
DYING	Psalm 23:4, Philippians 1:23, 2 Thessalonians 2:16-17, Jonah 2:7
PAIN	Romans 8:18, 2 Corinthians 4:17-18, 1 Peter 4:12, Revelation 21:4
LONELINESS	Isaiah 49:15, Hebrews 13:5, 8